Helen Hunt Jackson

Zeph

A Posthumous Story

Helen Hunt Jackson

Zeph
A Posthumous Story

ISBN/EAN: 9783744704564

Printed in Europe, USA, Canada, Australia, Japan

Cover: Foto ©Thomas Meinert / pixelio.de

More available books at **www.hansebooks.com**

A POSTHUMOUS STORY.

BY

HELEN JACKSON (H. H.),

AUTHOR OF

"RAMONA," "A CENTURY OF DISHONOR," "VERSES," "BITS OF TRAVEL,"
"BITS OF TRAVEL AT HOME," "BITS OF TALK ABOUT HOME
MATTERS," "BITS OF TALK FOR YOUNG FOLKS," "MERCY
PHILBRICK'S CHOICE," "HETTY'S STRANGE HISTORY,"
"NELLY'S SILVER MINE," "LETTERS FROM A CAT,"
"MAMMY TITTLEBACK AND HER FAMILY,"
"THE HUNTER CATS OF CONNORLOA."

———•———

BOSTON:
ROBERTS BROTHERS.
1885.

Z E P H.

I.

THE long Colorado twilight was over. But it was not yet quite lamplight time by the clock, and Miss Sophy Burr was sitting in a brown study at her kitchen window. This was the time she always took to make a swift retrospect in her mind of the results, profitable or otherwise, of the day just ended. She could think better in the dark, and the small economy of doing without a lamp until the last possible minute gave her a distinct pleasure. She was the strangest mixture of generosity and stinginess ever poured into human mould, her boarders said; and nobody knew better than they, for there was not a boarder in the house who had not been with her at least a year: some five and some six, and one old couple — Mr. and Mrs. Jones — had been with her ten. They were in Colorado for their health, — Mr. Jones for Mrs. Jones's, and *vice versa*, Mrs. Jones for Mr. Jones's; so they always declared, a rare instance of uniformity in conjugal needs. They began with Miss Sophy in the year when she began, and the town began, — almost before Miss Sophy fairly began; for all she had in way of a house then was a tent with a sort of fly attachment for a kitchen, and the boarders ate their meals in Miss Sophy's bedroom; or, to put it differently, Miss Sophy was obliged, owing to the scarcity of accommodations and the rush of custom, to sleep temporarily in her dining-room. That sounds better than to say that her boarders dined in her bedroom.

This was ten years ago. But to look at Pendar Basin to-day, and to recall what it was

then, one would say it must have been nearer
twenty, so marvellously had the colony grown
and developed. It was now what is called a
"thriving" place of some six thousand people, — all active, all making money, none rich,
none very poor, few of any pretence to what
is called in older places "social position," but
all or nearly all of fair intelligence and good
business education in their respective callings.

It had the making of a town in it, — a
superb site, good water, the command of two
mountain passes through which must go up and
out of the Basin all the freight for two large mining districts in the west and in the south. A
railroad, one of the main Colorado lines, brought
in the supplies to be thus shipped, and kept it,
moreover, in close relation with the outside world.
On the whole, a very lucky little village was
Pendar Basin; and especially lucky were those
who came in the beginning, in the "tent and
coyote" days, as they were called, and had seen

the lots they bought then for hundreds of dollars boom up into value rated by thousands.

Miss Sophy had not ten dollars in the world when she began. Her story was a sad one, but its details do not belong here. She had come out from New England to Colorado to join her lover; found him dead, buried only the week before her arrival, his last words full of anguished anxiety on her account, for he had not been successful, and had nothing to leave her except a grave to be tended; and the first thing the poor soul did, was to spend a few of her dollars in building a high fence around the bare sandy mound which hid her lover from her sight. Then she hired a tent, put out her sign, rolled up her sleeves, and went to work to earn money enough to carry her home. But the spell of the wilderness seized hold upon her, and she never went; and now there was not in all the town a better-known, a more universally respected woman than Miss Sophy: respected by the women because of her helpful cheery nature and exceeding decorum of conduct; respected by the men because she had a "level head" and "owned considerable property,"—surest passports to favor in the minds of business men.

As Miss Sophy sat revolving in her mind the relative proportions between what she had expended and what she had received on the day just closed, a frown deepened on her forehead. The balance did not please her. The margin of profit which she had prescribed to herself as a uniform rule had been diminished by injudicious luxury added to dinner.

"'T was the jelly," she said to herself. "That was what did it. But I can't bring myself to give roast mutton without it. Capers come cheaper and go farther. I'll boil oftener."

At least hundreds of times in the last eight years Miss Sophy had come to this or similar resolutions; but they always failed her when the instant arrived for putting them into practice.

Her love of a good dinner herself, and her still keener love of the approbation she won by setting it before others, kept up perpetual warfare with her savingness, and being two to one, often came off victorious, — often enough to keep up her reputation for setting the best table in the town; not often enough, however, to prevent her making money in the long run, and coming out at the end of the year with a creditable surplus ahead.

Just as Miss Sophy had said, half aloud, the last words of her soliloquy, she heard a faint knock at the door, — an irresolute, vacillating sort of knock, which aroused her curiosity at once.

"Who ever's that," she said, rising briskly, " that don't know his mind — or his fingers?" and she opened the door with impatient quickness.

A tall man, with a painful expression of incertitude and feebleness in his bent figure, stood before her without speaking.

"Well?" said Miss Sophy, sharply.

"I see a woman come in here a little while ago," he stammered, "'bout half an hour back."

"Well, supposin' you did!" interrupted Miss Sophy, still more sharply.

The man lifted his eyes to hers, with the look of a hunted animal. "Beg your pardon, ma'am, I did n't mean to 'fend ye; I thought mebbe 't was my wife, 'n' I 'd like to speak to her."

"Your wife!" cried Miss Sophy, eying him keenly, — she began to suspect him of being either a tramp or a lunatic, — "your wife! There has n't any woman come in here but me; 't was me came int' the gate just now. What 'd you think your wife was wantin' in here?"

The man hung his head. A strange hesitancy seemed to hold back his every word.

"She said she was goin' out to look for work," he said slowly, "an' I thought 't was her I see turnin' in here. Beg yor pardon, ma'am. Sorry I troubled ye."

"'Tain't any great trouble answerin' a question," replied Miss Sophy, her heart warming at once at the symptoms of suffering. "What sort of work did she want? What do you do? Do you want work?"

"I'm a carpenter," answered the man, still speaking slowly, and with almost a stumbling vagueness; "'t least that's my trade; I hain't got any tools now, though; I've been teamin' since I've been here."

"Do you want work?" asked Miss Sophy again, curtly.

No reply from the man. He seemed lost in thought, his eyes resting on Miss Sophy's face almost like the unseeing eyes of a sleep-walker.

"Man alive!" exclaimed Miss Sophy. "I'm askin' you if you want work! I can get you somethin' to do."

Still in the same curiously irresolute, hesitant voice the man answered: "No, I donno 's as

I do; that is, I donno's I'll be here; if I was here, I'd be glad o' work."

Miss Sophy's patience evaporated. "Well, you are here, 's near's I can judge; but you don't seem to me to want work so much's some men I've met. I don't know how you expect to get along in this world without workin'!"

" I don't," said the man. " 'Tain't that I ain't willin' to work. Ye hain't seen anything o' my wife, have ye?" he added, with a sudden desperate energy strangely unlike his manner hitherto. "She's somethin' your build, an' about your height; that was the reason I took you for her jest now; hain't no sech woman been here to-day? I've looked 'most everywhere else I could think of she'd be likely to go. Hain't she stopped here?"

" Stark crazy, evidently," thought Miss Sophy, as she answered: "No, she hasn't been here. No woman has been into this door to-day but me. Tell me where you live, and if your wife does call here I'll tell her you want to see her."

He started apprehensively. "Oh, no, ma'am," he said, "don't you say nothin' to her about it. She does n't like it to have me goin' round followin' her up. But I thought if she was in the house I'd like to get a word with her. My name's Riker, ma'am, — Zeph Riker. We live down in the Flat; ye can't miss it. If I'm here I'd be glad to do teamin'; or, if it was n't for not havin' tools, carpenterin' 's my trade. Goodnight, ma'am," and turning with a swift movement quite out of keeping with his shambling, inert attitude, he was gone.

Miss Sophy stood gazing out into the darkness after him for some seconds before she recovered from her bewilderment.

"Well, if that don't beat all the cur'us things that's ever come to my door yet!" she mentally ejaculated as she walked slowly through the kitchen into the dining-room and began setting her supper-table. "I guess he's crazy, poor thing! An' yet, he did n't seem somehow exactly like crazy neither. Perhaps some o' the folks'll know him. It's borne in on me that that man wants lookin' after."

None of the "folks," that is, Miss Sophy's boarders, had ever heard of Zeph Riker. As she told them the tale of her interview they all with one accord began to warn her against letting her sympathies go out towards him. He was a tramp; he was a burglar; he was a madman. One after another the boarders confidently advanced their theories of explanation of his singular behavior. It was odd to see, but a student of psychological phenomena could have classified the fact, how, as the conversation went on, Miss Sophy instinctively took the attitude of Zeph's defender.

"I don't b'leeve he's one o' them things," she said. "I ain't goin' to say it for sure, but I b'leeve he's jest kind o' dumb with trouble. I think that's all 't ails him, — some dreadful kind o' trouble; 'n' I think he ought to be looked after. It's been growin' on me, the more I've thought on 't, that 't was trouble he was in. Trouble makes folks that way some-times, — makes the words kind o' stick, an' your head seem to be all of a kind of a buzz, so you don't know anythin'. I think somebody ought to look after him."

Whenever it became clear to Miss Sophy that a thing or a person wanted "looking af-ter," the next logical step in her mind was the conclusion that she herself was the person whose duty lay in the line of that precise "look-ing after." "And especially after the trouble I've seen myself," said Miss Sophy, as she took her energetic way the next afternoon towards "The Flat," — a part of the town in which, strangely enough, she had never be-fore been. Miss Sophy was not a walker; that is, not an outdoor walker. The number of miles her tireless feet walked each day in her house it would have greatly surprised her to be told. She always said it tired her to death to walk, she was too stout; and when her "folks" sometimes observed, "Why, Miss Sophy, you are always walking, you never sit down," she would reply, "Oh, but I don't call it walkin', just runnin' round the house." And she honestly thought so; and felt over-fatigued by a half-hour's walk out of doors, when she would be fresh as a lark at the end of eight or nine hours' steady trot on her own floors.

It was a warm day, and the perspiration stood in drops on Miss Sophy's face when she finally found herself in the centre of the low, thinly settled district known as the Flat. Looking around her with mingled disgust and compassion, she indulged in the strongest ejaculation ever permitted to pass her lips.

"Land o' the livin'! What a hole! Poor creaturs! I don't suppose this land costs anythin', an' that's what brought 'em all in here. 'Tain't any more nor less than a kind o' cellar! A nice time scarlet fever'd have if it was to get in amongst these shanties. It's a shame! I never knew there was such a place 's this in this town. Well, one half the world does n't know how the other half lives, is jest as true in small places as in big, I vow! I don't know what the man meant by sayin' I could n't miss it. As if there was n't but one house in the Flat, and that his'n!" and Miss Sophy stood looking right and left in blank perplexity. The dogs and the children of the Flat soon gathered around her in wonder at her appearance, and from one of the oldest and least terrified of the children she learned which of the shanties was "Zeph's."

It was a poor little place, unfenced, uncared for, the house unpainted and dilapidated; and in strange mockery, it seemed, of the probable needs of the occupants of such a house, a trim new tying-post stood in front of the door. Looming up gauntly at its side was the half-done frame of a two-story house, evidently long since abandoned to wind and weather; for the beams were gray from exposure, and weeds grew high where floors should have been.

"Should n't wonder a mite if that was his'n," thought Miss Sophy. "He looked just the kind o' man to leave off that way. He wants spurrin' up." And there was an unconsciously authoritative quality in the very knock Miss Sophy gave at Zeph's door.

No answer. Again she knocked, still more sharply. No sound of any one stirring in the house. Impatiently Miss Sophy stepped to the window — there was but one — and looked in. An ejaculation of dismay escaped her.

"Of all the pigsties, for such a decent man as he looked, to be livin' in!" she said. It was indeed an unsightly place, — a bare floor, long unswept; a rusty cooking-stove in the centre of the room, ashes and brands piled on the hearth in front; a battered table; wooden chairs; a few utensils and dishes on cupboard shelves in one corner; through a half-open door into an adjoining room were to be seen untidy beds, and a bureau, with drawers wide open, looking as if they had just been ransacked by thieves; on a small stand at the head of the bed was a brass candlestick in which the candle had burned down to the socket, leaving grimy strata of melted tallow and blackened wick piled around it.

Miss Sophy's New England soul revolted.

"I donno's there's any use tryin' to help anybody that'd have a house like this," she thought, and stepped back from the window, again looking around her in a half-compassionate, half-resentful study of the region. As she did so she perceived a strange head peering over a high board fence just beyond the unfinished frame building. It was an old woman. Her thin gray hair, streaked with yellow, drawn up in a tight knot on the top of her head, was surmounted again by a pair of huge iron-rimmed spectacles of a kind out of vogue for fifty years. Her hair looked twenty years older than her face, and her face, again, twenty years older than her eyes, which were bright hazel, clear and keen, making the spectacles seem a grotesque adornment rather than a necessary aid to vision. The old woman had been watching Miss Sophy's every movement, and as she saw her turn away from the window, called out, "Ain't nobody in thar, be ther?"

"No," said Miss Sophy, "no one."

"I allowed he hed n't come hum," said the woman. "I seed thar warn't no smoke out'er'n ther chimbly, 'n' I said ter Vilm, sez I, 'I jest allow thet thar Zeph 's been walkin' ther streets all night, I allow he hez!'"

Miss Sophy walked briskly towards the fence. As she did so, the head disappeared from view, and simultaneously from behind the boards came the hospitable invitation, " Ef yeow 'll step raound ter the front a piece, I 'll let yer in ; this gate 's done nailed up, kase ther young uns 's allers lettin' ther pig aout."

" I never ! " thought Miss Sophy. " What next, I wonder ! " But she complied with the directions, and reaching the other side of the house found herself confronted by her strange interlocutor, who exclaimed, " Oh, ther yer be ! I allowed yer wan't comin', mebbe ! It took yer ser long, I allowed yer 'd gone off. Yer wuz lookin' for Zeph Riker, wuz n't yer ? Did yer want him ter work fur yer ? "

" Yes," replied the dazed Miss Sophy, who had never before heard the Missouri vernacular, and had never before seen so strange a figure as the one which now stood before her.

" Wall, thet 's jest what I wuz a hopin' up when I seed yer gwine ter ther door. I allowed to myself thet Zeph wuz gwine ter git holped ;

he's clar down, Zeph is, 'n' I allow he'll jest git ter be outer'n his wits ef he keeps on ther way he's ben goin', er walkin', walkin', night-times 'n' daytimes; they's all one ter him, he sez, an' she ain't wuth it, 'n' never wuz. Thar's lots kin tell him thet; but he won't listen to nary word agen her, nary. Vilm, he 'lows he's crazy, naow; but I don't. He's got's wits, Zeph hez; an' there wan't never no better man cum inter this yer flairt, never. I allow ter you ther warn't. He's reel good, Zeph is. I ain't gwine ter say but what ther's men thet's rustled more'n he did; but 't ain't in some men *to* rustle; thar's some that ken, an' thar's some that can't; an' thar can't nobody rustle when ther heart's took outer 'em; 'n' thet's what's ther matter with Zeph; he's got the heart gone plumb outer him; he's been settin' thar 'n thet house sence she's went off this last time, 'n' I allow he'd ha' starved ter death ef I hedn't tuk him over vittles. We're pore, but we ain't gwine ter see a human critter starve, not right next dore, we ain't. I seed him when he went off yesterday mornin'. I was jest cummin' crost ther floor, an' I seed him kinder stealin' by. He know'd I'd ask him whar he wuz gwine. An' sez I, 'Zeph Riker, air yer goin' huntin' thet woman agen? I allow yer the biggest fool in all this yer flairt, Zeph Riker.' Thet's what I said. I hain't no patience with a man that'll git down 'n' be run over wuss 'n ary dog. An' he jest give me sech er look, an' he sez, 'She's my wife, Gammer! an', more'n somever, she's took the chillen along this time.' 'She hain't!' sez I. 'Yes, she hez,' sez he. Wall, when I heered she'd got the chillen, I hed n't no more ter say. He'd got ter go hunt 'em, 'n' git 'em away ef he ennywise could; fur 't's a dumb shame fur little chillen to be with a — sech a critter's she is!" And Gammer Stein stopped at last, not for lack of words, but of breath.

"I don't know what you're talkin' about,"

was Miss Sophy's sole reply to this outpouring of mingled invective and sympathy.

"Don't know what I'm talkin' abaout!" cried the old woman, wrathfully. "Hain't you heered haow Zeph Riker's wife's allers gwine off 'n' leavin' him? Sometimes 't is one thing, 'n' sometimes 't is another; she's allers got an excuse ready; most gen'ully it's lookin' fur work, she sez; she lets on she's got ter support the family, 'n' she's allers a scandalizin' him up 'n' down; she 'lows he don't yern nothin', 'n' she sez ef one don't bring in, the other must; 'n' so she goes off ter work down 'n the restaurants, fust one, 'n' then another, but 's allers 'n the one whar that skunk o' a feller she's goin' with, thet Nat Leeson, 's a cookin'. Thet's the kind o' work she's a doin'! I allow she'd oughter be took up; she'd oughter; sech women's a disgrace to thar sex, they air now. Hain't yeow heered nothin' abaout it? I allow yeow must be a stranger hyar, ef yeow hain't heered o' Rusha Riker. She's jest famed, ill famed, too, in this hyar town. I allowed thar warn't nobody thet hed n't heered o' her scandaliginous carak'ter!"

This last adjective was too much for Miss Sophy's risibles. In spite of herself she laughed; at which Gammer Stein broke out again: "I allow 'tain't no larfin' marter; it's jest life 'n' death, thet's what 't is, to this hyar man 'n' his chillen, 'n' ef thar ain't murder in't afore all's said 'n' done, I allow we kin be thankful t' ther A'mighty. What wuz ye wantin' o' Zeph, ef so be 's ye never heered o' him afore?" And pulling down her spectacles, and adjusting them perilously near the end of her nose, Gammer Stein looked scrutinizingly across their iron rims at her visitor. "I don't know ye," she said distrustfully. "What mought yer name be? Be ye new cum?"

"Oh, no," replied Miss Sophy. "I have lived here ever since the town was begun; but I live a mile away from here, and I have never happened to hear of Zeph till yesterday, when he came to my house lookin' for his wife. I thought he was in some sort of trouble, an' I'd look after him a little."

"Jes so, jes so," said Gammer, instantly appeased by the presence of sympathy. "Yer live on ther hill, I allow?"

"Yes," said Miss Sophy.

"Land's drefful dear up thar," replied Gammer, "or else me 'n' Vilm, we'd been up thar tew, yeow bet! I did n't never like hollers; but pore folks's got ter live whar they kin. Back 'n Missouri we wuz up on a ridge like, but 't warn't ser healthy 's this, fur all 't wuz higher; 'n' Vilm 's allers tellin' me thet this hyar flairt ain't reelly a holler. Thar can't be no hollers, he sez, when ther hull country's ez high up ez this is; but I tell him I don't want ter live 'n enny place thet ser much 's favors ther look 'v er holler, 'n' 's soon 's we

git er little erhead we 's got ter move outer'n
this flairt. What part o' ther hill der yeow live
on? Be yeow a married woman?"

"No," replied Miss Sophy, curtly, with something in her tone which the sensitive old
woman felt without fully recognizing, and instinctively wished she had not asked the question. " I have never been married. I live
alone. I keep the boarding-house next to the
Presbyterian church."

"Dew yer?" exclaimed Gammer. "Naow
I allow thet's kind o' cur'us. Vilm, he's done
teamin' ter yeour place; he's tolt me abaout
yeow. Don't yer want er man steady ter dew
yer outside work? Ef ye'd take Zeph in, he's
handy; he's a fust-rate carpenter tew, 'n' a good
hand fur hosses; ef he'd jest git hisself inter some
sech place, thar's plenty'd take keer o' the chillen for jest their keep, 'n' thay're li'le, 't would
n't be much, 'n' let thet hussy o' his'n go
whar she belongs; 'n' I allow thar ain't much

doubtin' whar 't 'd be. Ef he cud wunst git shet
'v her wunst fur all, thar 'd be some hope o'
Zeph yit. He wuz a reel likely man when they
fust moved in hyar three years ago. She
wan't what she oughter be, neow I don't
s'pose; but she had n't gin herself clean away
t' the devil then 's she hez sence. I allow it 's
strange yer hain't never heered o' her. Why,
she 's been up inter the jail, 'n' her name 'n
the paper, 'n the 'Times,' 'n' the trial, 'n' all.
Jerushy Riker 'disorderly' they called it; 'n'
Zeph he paid the fine, 'n' all the costs, 'n' got
her hum; 'n' I allow ter yeow 't wan't more 'n
a week 'fore she wuz aout agen, 'n' feathers 'n
her bunnit, 'n' goin' to dances wi' thet Nat, 's
brazhen 's any brass ye ever seen. 'N' there
was n't erry woman 'n this flairt 'ud ser much
's speak ter her, only ther men. I allow men
is shameful; 'n' 's long 's they 'll go with her
'n' give her things, she just spites the women.
My man won't hev nothin' ter say ter her; he

sez he'd kill her ef she wuz his'n, 'n' I sh'd hope he would. But thet ther Zeph, he jest worships her, 's ef she wuz the best wife a man ever hed. He'll foller her, 'n' coax her, 'n' hang round her, 'n' give her his last cent he's got in this blessed yarth, ef she'll only look wunst torerds him."

" He's a fool ! " broke in Miss Sophy.

"Wall, yis, I allow he is," said Gammer, reflectively. " I allow he must be; an' yit he ain't, nuther. Zeph ain't no fool. Ef a man gits took thet way 'bout a woman, he can't holp hisself, 'thout he kin git shet 'v her outern out. Thet's what I'm tellin' him allers. I sez to him jest this last week, sez I, ' Zeph Riker, yeow jest light aout er hyar; yeow take yer team,' — he's got a fust-rate team ef he hain't sold 'em since last week to git money 'n' go hunt fur thet hussy, — 'yeow take yeour team 'n' ther young uns, 'n' light aout; 'n' yeow keep er travellin' till yer've got whar yer can't never hear name of her agin. Yeow kin stop when your money's giv aout, 'n' work till yer git more ter go on with; 'n' yeow jest keep movin'. I allow Californy'd be fur enough; 'n' livin' 's easy made thar, everybody sez thet's ben thar; yeow jest light aout er hyar.'"

"What did he say?" asked Miss Sophy, breathlessly.

" He did n't say but jest tew words, he did n't," replied Gammer. "But them tew, 'n' the way he sed 'em, wuz more 'n some folks's preachin' all day. He sez, sez he, 'Gammer, I can't;' 'n' I allow to yeow I 'spect thet's jest the trew on't; 'n' ef he can't, he can't."

"You don't mean to tell me you think he loves the woman still!" cried Miss Sophy.

"But he doos," said Gammer. " Thet's why Vilm sez he's a fool, 'n' I can't gainsay 't he ain't; 'n' yit thar's times, I allow to yeow, when I git ter feelin' 's ef he wuz better 'n most folks. He don't never give her a hash word; he's

allers 's glad ter see her 's aour pup hyar ter see
the chillen cumin' hum when school 's aout; 'n'
he 'll slave hisself ter death, 'n' sell the coat
offen his back, ter git her all she wants; 'n' she
don't give him ser much 's a word er a look, let
alone disgracin' him 'n' his chillen 'n' the name
he 's gin her! I donno 's the Lord 's gwine ter
call him a fool er not. It kind o' cums over me
cur'us sometimes, ther way he acts." And the
old woman gazed half-inquiringly, half-shame-
facedly, into Miss Sophy's face.

Miss Sophy's eyes were full of tears. She
tried to keep them back, but they were too big
to be concealed, — genuine, unmistakable tears.
Brushing them away impatiently, she said,
"Well, he 's a fool, anyhow!"

"I s'pose he must be," replied Gammer.
"Thar ain't many like him."

"I wonder where he is now," said Miss Sophy.

"No knowin'," said Gammer. "It 's two days
naow he 's ben huntin' her. He won't go in

bold like 'n' ask ef she's thar 't these places,
kase it mads her. He'll jest hang raound 'n'
watch. He sez he won't mortify her! Him
mortify her! Thet sounds likely, don't it?
He sed thet ter me wunst, when I sed ter
him, sez I, 'Zeph Riker, ef yer want her ser
bad's yer say, take er perliceman 'n' go git her.
She's yer wife. The law guvs her ter ye where
somever yer kin ketch her.' 'I would n't mortify her thet way,' sez he; 'n' then I jest up 'n' I
sez ter him — wall, I pollergized ter him arter
fur the words I used; they wuz outrageous, 'n'
ther would n't nobody but a fool ha' stood 'em,
Vilm sed; but somehow, I allow ter yeow, I've
allers liked him better sence thet day. Sez he,
'I don't feel ter blame yer, not fur nothin' yer
say. Thar can't nobody understand, but I can't
holp myself.'"

Strange emotions were tugging at Miss
Sophy's heart-strings. What had this poor
man's experiences in common with hers?

Nothing, surely. The lover she had lost had been an upright man. Her affection had never been put to the strain of wrestling with even so much as a suspicion of the unworthiness of its object. And if such evil destiny as that had ever befallen her, she would have seemed to be the last person, — she with her practical common sense, clear business head, matter-of-fact way of looking at life, — the last person, surely, to have clung to a base and dishonored man. And yet this pathetic story she was hearing of Zeph Riker's inalienable affection for the miserable creature he called wife seemed to be breaking up within her bosom the very foundations of some strange, undreamed-of, mighty emotion which threatened to overwhelm her.

"I don't know what's the matter with me," thought Miss Sophy. "It must be the long walk. It always does upset me to walk."

"I must be going now," she said suddenly. "I have a great deal to do. I wish you'd let

me know if there is anything I can do to help
this poor man. If he wants work I can give
him a good deal." And she turned abruptly
away, to the great discomfiture of Gammer
Stein, who had not said half her say.

"Ye'll call raound agen, won't ye?" she
called after her. "Dew. I'd like ter see yer
fust-rate."

"Perhaps I will," said Miss Sophy, "some
day. But I'm very busy. You must come and
see me."

This pleased Gammer even better.

"I allow I will," she said eagerly. "I'd like
ter see yer place. I wuz by thar. It's an awful
nice house yer got."

"Good afternoon," said Miss Sophy, already
some paces away, and quickening her steps to
avoid further talk. She walked unconsciously
faster and faster till she reached home. Not
for ten years had Miss Sophy's spinster breast
been the seat of such keen and conflicting

emotion. She could neither analyze it nor shake it off. The image of her long-buried lover rose up before her with almost terrifying vividness, and she seemed compelled by some strange power outside of herself to continue thinking of him, fancying what would have been the result had their marriage taken place and he afterward proved as unfit for trust, unworthy of love, as Zeph's wife. She felt herself disloyal at the very thought, but she could not free herself from it.

"What nonsense!" she said to herself, sternly. "There was n't a bad drop of blood in Robert Barrett's veins, not one; not a man in that family ever went to the bad."

"But what if he had?" persisted this strangely disquieted spirit in her breast. "What if he had? What if he had been overpowered by temptation? He was human. Men seemingly as good as he have fallen; have become drunk-ards; have been unfaithful to their wives.

What if he had? What would you have done?
Would n't you have clung to him through everything? Do you suppose you could ever have
left off loving him, no matter what he had
done?"

"No, I know I could n't," responded Miss
Sophy's passionate heart, also strangely disquieted in her breast; "I know I could n't!"

And then by a not unnatural sequence there
came into her thoughts the solemn words of the
marriage service, which she could never hear
without a strange pang, remembering that she
had once expected to hear them spoken for
herself. "'For better, for worse; till death do
us part.' What does that mean," she said, "if
it does not mean just what this poor Zeph
is doing? 'For better, for worse,' no matter
how much worse! I do believe I should have
looked at it just as he does, this very minute!
I would n't wonder if I'd ha' been just such a
fool 's he is; an' I don't know as I call it exactly

bein' a fool, neither, any more 'n she does!" And with a tremendous effort Miss Sophy shook herself free from the bootless soliloquy, and went about her work, reiterating in her mind the original resolution with which she had left home early in the afternoon, — that that man must be "looked after."

II.

WHEN Zeph left Miss Sophy's door he had in his mind no specific plan of action, although from his brisk gait one would have supposed him to have in view a definite goal which he wished to reach in the shortest possible time. He walked on, looking neither to the right nor the left, till he reached the outskirts of the town, at the farthest possible remove from his own house. Here the land fell away abruptly into bottoms through which ran a stream, low and shrunken now from the long drought. The sight of the water was the first thing which roused him from the vague yet painful reverie in which he had been walking. As he looked into the water, he thought to himself, " If it was 's high 's I 've seen it in the spring freshets, I believe I'd jump in and make an end o' this misery. Perhaps 't would be better for her if I was out o' the world altogether. But a fellow 'd have to hold himself down, to drown in that depth o' water." And with a dreary smile at the thought he turned back towards the town. Suddenly a new idea struck him.

"Mebbe she's gone home now, an' she 'll be worse 'n ever, not findin' any fire nor nothin' to cook. I'll go home an' clear up, and get some steak!" He put his hand in his pocket and drew out the few bits of money he had there, — less than two dollars in all. He sighed bitterly as he looked at it. "Come to that, has it, an' I hain't bought a mouthful to eat to-day! Don't take long to play a man out, lying by this way. But there's enough for a good supper to-night!" And he quickened his pace.

How many times had he made just such bootless returns as this, each time lured on by a stronger and stronger hope that surely now she would have come back; he would see a light at the window telling him she was there; she must have come by this time! And each time it had been only a delusion; each time the empty, silent house and the cold, blackened hearth had mocked his misery anew, and he had turned away sicker at heart, more despairing than ever, to resume his hopeless quest.

"She likes beefsteak better 'n anythin' else," he said to himself as he entered the streets once more and looked on the brightly lighted shops on either hand. "I 'll get a first-rate good one; and there 's a bit o' horse-radish left in the tumbler; she likes that." And as he went on with his foolish, affectionate plannings, the hope in his bosom grew stronger, till he half persuaded himself that he knew she was at home waiting for him to bring the supper, or that his thus making ready for her would bring her before long. And yet he had done this very thing, hoped this unreasoning hope, scores of times before, all in vain. Why did he still continue to hope? He could not have told.

As he paid for the meat the butcher, eying him closely, said, "All well at home, Riker?"

Zeph gave a slight start, but recovering himself instantly, replied, "Thank you; I hope so. Hain't been home since mornin'."

"Don't that beat all?" said the butcher, after he had gone, turning to his assistant. "Nobody's never heard Zeph Riker admit it yet when his wife's run off from him an' he's a huntin' her; an' he don't never exactly lie about it neither. He's always got his answer ready."

"He's a blamed fool he don't bill her," said the assistant.

"That's so," replied the other. "A little teched in the upper story, I reckon. But he's a good fellow's ever lived; an' she's a handsome huzzy. I expect he can't let go on her."

"Well, I 'd let go on her mighty quick if she b'longed to me. I know that! I say he 's a blamed fool!" replied the assistant, waxing wrathy. "Why, she 's been took up, 'n' in jail. She was down to the beer-garden with that Nat 'n' a lot o' others, 'n' they all got tight, 'n' kicked up such a row the night watchman clapped the hull batch of 'em into the lock-up; 'n' Riker he went right into court 'n' paid everything, 'n' got her out 'n' took her home. She might ha' rotted there for all me, if I 'd been her husband."

"When ye 've got a wife o' your own, mebbe ye 'll know more 'n you do now," said the butcher, going to the door and looking after Zeph's figure, now nearly lost in the darkness. "He 's a streakin' it like lightnin'. I do believe the fellow thinks she 's to home waitin' for him."

"Where is she?" asked the assistant.

"Out on the mesa, in them freighters' camp,"

replied the butcher. "She's been there three days, cookin' for 'em, 'n' trainin' like Sam Hill. I tell you she's a flyer! But she can cook, you bet. Tim was in to-day buyin' veal 'n' a turkey. He said they was goin' to keep Sunday in that camp, and no mistake! they'd got Rusha Riker for cook and Sal Leeson for preacher! If Riker'd ever ask anybody where she's gone to, he'd find out a heap quicker 'n he does. But he's too proud. He never opens his head to nobody, an' there ain't nobody goin' to volunteer to tell him; 'n' so he goes sozzlin' round, 'n' wastin' his time, 'n' gettin' out o' pocket. I hain't much patience with him myself, I own; but I don't know how we'd any of us act if we was placed just 's he is. It's pretty hard tellin'."

As Zeph drew near his home he walked faster. The more he thought, the surer he felt she would be there; the more he blamed himself for not having had everything ready for her at early dusk. "I might ha' remembered," he said to himself remorsefully, "that its bein' Saturday night 'd be likely to bring her home, for she hain't took none o' her best things nor the youngsters', an' of course she'll come back to get 'em even if she don't stay." And he broke into a run at the top of the hill above the Flat walling it to the west. Twinkling lights like fireflies shone all over the place; the humble homes there were thick set; a rush of emotion came over Zeph as he saw the glimmering lights. "All them homes," he thought, "an' not one of 'em 's got such trouble 's I have! God! but it's hard!" And he pressed on, newly disheartened, as so many lonely souls have been, by the simple sight of home-lights gleaming.

As he turned the corner, where, if a light were burning in his own window it would greet his eye, his heart beat loud. "If she ain't there this time I think it'll kill me!" he muttered.

All was dark. She was not there. He stopped, gazed, threw down his parcels on the ground, and folded his arms on his breast. The moon was just coming up in the east, beyond the wide plains which stretched away, it seemed endlessly. Zeph looked at it with dogged dislike. "I don't need no moonlight to-night," he thought. "I forgot 't was full moon. I might ha' known she would n't come home early if 't was full moon. She's foolin' somewhere."

The moon came up fast; its white light fell on the beams of the unfinished frame, which stood mute record of the terrible ruin of all Zeph's plans and hopes of a home. The outlines of the building loomed out against the sky like a black skeleton, and smote Zeph's very heart. "Just about 's much home 's I 've got," he said to himself. "A kind of a ghost it looks like, in this light, 'n' that 's about what it is! I believe I 'll take the thing down. The lumber 'd bring considerable. But she 'll throw it up at me if I do; she's always blamin' me for not finishin' it. I guess most folks 'd say the house she 's got 's good enough to run away from!" And Zeph strode on gloomily, with reluctant steps.

Entering the house, he looked around the room with a bitter expression on his face. "I 've a mind to clear out too," he thought. "What's the use o' goin' on this way? But, no, I can't. I can't leave her so long 's there 's a chance o' gettin' her right. She did care for me once, I know she did; an' she is real fond o' the children; there can't nobody say she does n't love them even if she has got so set against me; an' if she had n't got some good heart somewhere she 'd hate them too just because I 'm their father. I 've heard o' women's turnin' thet way till they could n't bide the sight o' husband nor children, either one o' them. It 's a kind o' craziness comes over 'em. Poor Rushy! Seems 's if she must be crazy."

While thinking these thoughts he was mechanically moving about the rooms, setting things into place, putting back the tumbled clothes into the drawers, making the beds; then he lighted a fire in the stove, and opening the drawer in the table took out a fresh candle and set it in the candlestick. "That's the last but one," he said, "but I'll light it, an' then if she does come in, she'll know I'll be back before long."

He put the beefsteak on a platter by the candlestick. "So she'll see it first thing," he thought, "an' know I got something good for supper."

Then he went out, locking the door and putting the key in their usual hiding-place for it, — a hollow under the tying-post.

The thought of the freighters' camp had at last occurred to him, and he could not rest now till he had found out if his wife were there. He groaned aloud as he turned his steps toward the mesa.

"I'd 'most as soon find her dead," he thought, "as find her there! Don't know but I'd sooner! If she's been there all this time, 't ain't for no good. But then she's got the children along. She wouldn't—" And Zeph clenched his hands and groaned again.

The "mesa" was a high table-land stretching away to the north of the town, not over a quarter of a mile wide on the top. Its sides were broken up into alternating shallow cañons and soft rounding ridges, grass-grown,—good places for grazing and shelter; at the base of the western side ran a little brook. It was a favorite spot for camping, and at times in the summer looked like an army encampment, so thickly dotted was it with white tents and wagons and picketed horses.

"It's the strangest thing I never thought

4

o' that before!" mused Zeph as he struck out into the plain. "They'll pay good wages to a cook, the boys will, when they're in town; and Rushy can't be beat at cookin', that's one thing." And he tried manfully to keep out all other interpretations of her presence there. "If so be's she's here," he reiterated to himself, "I'm a dumb fool to cry out 'fore I know I'm hurt worse 'n I am by just not knowin' what's got her."

The moon was riding high in the heavens and flooding plain, mesa, mountains, all, with a light hardly less clear than sun, as Zeph finally climbed up through one of the shorter cañons and came out on the top of the mesa. The freighters' camp was close before him, — so close that he started, and involuntarily retreated a step or two into cover of the ridge, lest he should be too suddenly seen. There was but one tent. From that came sounds of fiddling and riotous laughter.

"She's there, for sure!" sighed Zeph. "Lord have mercy on me! Has she got them children in there this time o' night?" and he glanced up at the moon. "Ten o'clock if it's a minute! The poor young uns!"

There were ten of the freight-wagons arranged in a circle around the tent, some of them with rounded white tops. Cautiously Zeph stole up to one of these, parted the flaps at the back, and looked in. Surely his fatherly instinct had guided him to the spot. There lay his two children sound asleep on a straw bed in the bottom of the wagon. Surprise, joy, anguish, all held Zeph dumb. As he stood looking at them the boy raised his head and opened his eyes.

"Pappy, pappy!" he cried, and scrambled towards him, rousing the baby, who began to whimper.

"Hush, sis, hush!" he exclaimed. "Mammy said she'd whip ye if ye cried! It's pappy!

Don't ye know pappy?" In a second more the little creature was in her father's arms, and for a brief moment Zeph felt himself glad. Only for a moment, however.

"Zephie," he said, "where's your mammy?"

"In there," replied the child, pointing towards the tent. "There's a lot o' men in there; they're dancin'; the men's beds is all took out."

"Who's there besides mammy? any other women besides mammy?" asked Zeph, his words stifling him as he spoke them.

"Nobody but Sal," replied Zephie. "She's here all the time to help mam cook. Mam says she never cooked so much vittles before. Mam reckons they must ben starved where they come from. Splendid vittles, pap, they has! It's bully! Why didn't you come too, pap? Mam was tellin' some o' the men she was a lookin' for ye to come 'fore now."

Bitter gall and wormwood to the father's ears

were these innocent prattlings of his boy. Too
well he knew the gibe and jest with which his
wife had told " some of the men " she was looking for him to appear on the scene. Too well
he knew the " Sal " who was her assistant, —
one of the most notorious women in the town,
and sister of the man to whom Zeph still persuaded himself he owed all the misery which
had come into his married life. He was mistaken. Nat Leeson was merely one man among
many who had had right to mock at his dishonor; but it was Nat Leeson with whom his
wife's relations were now openly and flaunt-
ingly intimate. It was Nat Leeson for whom
she really cared, so far as it was in her
shallow, unprincipled nature to care for any
man.

"We're comin' home to-morrow, pap," continued Zephie; " mam says she's tired out; 'n'
the teams is all goin' to start up the mountains
early Monday mornin'; so mam 'n' Sally's goin'

to cook up lots o' vittles to-morrow for 'em to take, 'n' then we 're comin' home."

"Be ye? That's good!" said Zeph. "You tell mammy pap 's real glad ye 're comin' home, will ye?"

"Stay, pap," replied the boy. "You stay, too; there 's lots room in here. Sal and mam and us all sleeps in here. You stay; we 're goin' to have turkey to-morrow, — an awful big one."

"No, I can't stay, my boy," replied Zeph. "Mammy 's too busy. She don't want me. You help her all you can, Zephie, an' you be sure 'n' tell her pap was here, 'n' he was dreadful glad you was all comin' home to-morrow, will ye? Tell her pap 's ben dreadful lonesome. Don't ye forget now to tell her 's soon 's she comes to bed."

"I 'll tell her 'n the mornin'," said Zephie. "I 'll be asleep when she comes to bed."

"No, you tell her to-night, Zephie," said

his father. "You stay awake till she comes. She'll be here pretty soon, I guess. It's late now."

"Well, I'll try," said the child; "but, pap, I'll be awful sleepy 's soon 's you're gone. Why don't you go up 'n' speak to her in the tent ?"

"Oh, I don't want to interrupt the dancing!" said poor Zeph. "I don't know any o' the men."

"Yes, Nat's there! you know him," said the child. "All the rest is freighters."

This was the last drop in unhappy Zeph's cup. It overflowed.

"I'll — " he began in a loud tone. "No, I won't either," he continued; and kissing the baby, who had nestled herself to sleep in his arms, he laid her gently down on the straw, and then kissing the boy, said, "Good-night, Zephie; be a good boy, and take care of your little sister. Good-night; I must go now." And as cautiously as he had come, he stole down the cañon and was gone.

Skirting along the base of the mesa for some rods, he climbed up again at a point some distance the other side of the tent, where stood a clump of huge pine-trees. Seating himself on the ground, partially hid by the trunk of the largest of these trees, he fixed his eyes on the tent. Now that he knew his wife was there, he would watch the place all night. It appeared to him that the moon stood still in the sky, so long did the moments seem before the freighters' revelry broke up. At last, with loud laughing and talking, the party came out from the tent and separated for the night: the men going to their respective wagons, and his wife and Sal — with what breathless anguish he watched their every step! — to the wagon in which the children lay. Soon the lights were all out, and the stillness, the unutterable wilderness stillness, rested on the place. Zeph drew a long breath of relief. " That's over!" he said aloud, and leaned his head back against the tree.

He had eaten nothing since morning, but he was not conscious of hunger or faintness. He had been under such a mental strain that all physical sensations were dulled. He could not have told, had he been asked, when he last ate food. Matters seemed to him to be fast approaching a crisis in his life; he felt a vague terror of he knew not what, — some terrible catastrophe approaching. He had felt this fear-stricken presentiment growing within him rapidly during the last three days. None of his previous experiences of suffering in consequence of his wife's conduct had so told upon him. No one of her unexplained or only too well explained absences from home had crushed him like this last one. As he sat hour after hour in this strange solitude, alone, as it almost seemed, in the universe, with the vast star-set dome of the sky above him and

the vast rayless plains stretching around him,
the near mountains looming up colossal and
black like an eternal barrier in the west, he
lived these absences all over again in full and
harrowing detail.

The first one, — that was three years ago.
How well he recollected his fright when he
found her gone; the angry incredulity with
which he heard Gammer Stein's half-implied
reflection on her character that night; the joy
with which he welcomed her back the next
morning, and the full acceptance he had given
to her story of having been watching with the
sick child of a neighbor, the child too sick to
be left, and no one in the house who could be
sent with a message to him. It was not many
weeks before he knew that this was a shameful, shameless lie. And after that miseries had
thickened in his life, — his own house a gather-
ing-place of the disgraceful and the disgraced;
his wife oftener and oftener absent, sometimes

with excuse, sometimes without; her intimate associates men and women with whom no self-respecting person would consort; his earnings wasted on fineries or worse.

"It's been just a hell on earth, that's what it's been," he thought, as he buried his face in his hands at some of the reminiscences. That brief interval of quiet of a few months during which the last child had been born, — the little girl from whose unconscious influence over the mother's heart he had hoped much, — recurred to him now, in this bitter retrospect, merely as an intensification of his woe. "And me hopin' its bein' a girl might maybe save her! I don't see why I thought that'd make any difference if the boy didn't!"

How vividly he recalled the day when they were discussing the baby's name; and his wife having expressed the desire to give it her own name, he had taken heart from that, and said to her meaningly, "Would ye really like to have her called by your name, Rushy?" and she, in her usual flippant tone, and yet he fancied with a shade of feeling in her face, had answered, " You 've got the boy named for you, an' I should think the girl ought to be named for me; that 's no more 'n fair;" and he had made haste to reply, " Of course 't ain't, an' I 'd rather call her Rushy than any other name 'n all the world, 'n' you know that, wife, without my tellin' ye; 'n' she 's goin' to favor you in looks, too; anybody with half an eye can see that a'ready; so there 'll be two Rushy Rikers the first thing ye know." And when he said this his wife colored, and said, " I hope to goodness she 'll turn out better 'n the first Rushy Riker!" And he, poor fool, had gone about for many a week hugging that exclamation to his soul as an omen and token of good coming to their lives. But it was short-lived. Before her baby was three months old the old demons of love of admiration, excitement, finery, folly, and sin

had got full hold again of her weak and un-
stable nature, and all was as bad as before,
or worse.

Then came the most flagrant of all her mis-
demeanors, — the drunken frolic at the beer-garden and the disgrace of the lock-up; and after
that all sense of shame or of restraint seemed to
leave her; and finally, only a few weeks ago, the
most daring of all her escapades, when, taking
the baby, she had gone to Denver openly in
the company of Nat Leeson and his sister;
then it was that Zeph, at his wits' end, had sold
some of their furniture and his kit of carpenter's tools to get money for the journey, put
the boy into Gammer Stein's motherly keeping,
followed and tracked her; and for the first and
only time exercising his husbandly authority over
her, had brought her home. But it was only
an enforced return. She was sullen, reluctant,
full of hatred and reproaches. "A pretty home
it was," she said, "to bring a woman back to,

stripped of half the furniture, and not a dollar to buy anything with!" If he'd let her alone, she'd make her own living an' not be beholden to anybody.

"Hold your tongue, Rushy!" cried Zeph, the only time in his life he had thus spoken to her. "Don't you dare to talk to me about makin' your own livin'! If you'll stay at home an' keep decent, I'll keep ye in as good a livin' as folks o' our station needs! I'd ha' had a good house done for ye now, if ye'd done's ye'd oughter."

"It's easy makin' excuses," she retorted; "ye never did have no spunk, an' it's a mighty poor livin' ye'll ever get in this world. I donno what's hendered your buildin' the house 'fore now, 'cept your own laziness!"

"I'll tell ye what's hendered me, Rushy," replied Zeph, thoroughly angered, — "runnin' round all creation huntin' you, 'n' sellin' my tools to get money to follow ye an' keep ye from

comin' on the town! That's what's hendered
me; an' 't will hender me, too, s' long's ye go
on as ye're doin'!"

As Zeph lived over this bitterest of all their
quarrels his heart smote him remorsefully.

"I expect I was too fierce with her," he
thought. "Perhaps if I'd been real lovin' then
she'd ha' come round. She's been lots worse
ever since then, 'n' I expect I did n't manage
right. I'll try 'n' see if I can't be different to
her to-morrow when she comes home. She's
had the children along with her this time, 'n'
that's some comfort."

It was near morning when Zeph finally fell
into an uneasy sleep. His sorrows pursued him
even there, and he dreamed a nightmare dream
of seeing his wife at the window of a burning
house and being unable to move hand or foot
to her rescue. He opened his eyes with the
horror of this dream full upon him, and for the
first second thought the dream was no dream,

but actual truth; for the sky over his head and
the whole front of the mountain range on his
right were red as from the light of a conflagra-
tion. Bewildered, he sprang to his feet with a
cry, but in the same second sank down again,
saying, " It 's only the sun a comin' up! Lord!
How it scared me! "

It was the marvellous rosy dawn peculiar
to high altitudes. So vivid, so fiery a glow·
does it spread over both sky and earth for
a few seconds before sunrise, that when the
sun is above the horizon, and the day fairly
breaks, the light seems less, and not more, and
the earth and sky darkened instead of illu-
mined.

All was still in the freighters' camp. A few
faint upward curls of smoke in the distant town
were the only signs of life in the beautiful land-
scape. As Zeph gazed on the picture he felt
insensibly strengthened.

" 'T don't seem 's if folks need to suffer so 'n

such a world 's this," he thought; "things must come out right, sooner or later, somehow, if there 's any kind o' reason 'n anything. It don't look no ways likely that God set it all a goin' jest to make folks miserable! I expect it 's all our own fault, somewheres, if things goes wrong! I believe Rushy 'n' I 'll get on yet. If I could once rake 'n' scrape money enough to take her clean out o' this place 'n' begin over again, that would be best; but how to fetch that about I don't see!"

Time slipped by imperceptibly to Zeph absorbed in his reverie, and an hour or more had gone, when he was roused by the sounds of stirring in the camp. Hastily concealing himself in a ravine, he lay stretched along the ground, only his eyes above the edge of the mesa, and watched every movement. He saw his wife and Sal come out, the children following, the fires lighted in the camp stoves, the preparations for cooking begun. Presently he saw Nat Leeson stroll up towards the stoves and stop to talk with his sister.

"If I see him go nigh Rushy I'll do some harm, I know I shall," said Zeph. "I'll not risk it. I'll leave here." And darting down the ravine he set off by a circuitous route, on which he could not be seen, towards home.

When he reached the outskirts of the town the church-bells were ringing. The sound seemed full of unwonted invitation to Zeph. It was long since he had been inside the walls of a church. In the first years of their married life Rushy had been fond of going to meeting of a Sunday, and he had been only too proud to go with her and see the admiration with which people looked at her handsome face and pretty clothes. Even then were to be seen, if Zeph had only had the wisdom to recognize them, the germs of all the misery and shame which time had since brought. But he looked on with the blinded eyes of a man's first unreasoning passion, saw nothing wrong, thought no harm, feared no evil. He even shared the pride, which seemed innocent, in the undeniable fact that Rushy was the handsomest woman in the congregation. And now, alas, it was for Rushy's sake, and because of her beauty, that he was ashamed to look any man in the eye!

A strange desire seized him to go this morning and hear what the preacher had to say. He looked down at his clothes. They were shabby enough, certainly; not at all what he would once have thought it necessary to wear to be decent at church. But Zeph had been down into depths from which all thoughts of trivial considerations had long ago vanished. He smiled half sadly as he turned towards the church door, saying to himself, "I would n't have been caught goin' to meetin' in such cloes 's these once; but I guess it don't make any difference to nobody but me, 'n' I feel a real call to hear some hymn-singin' to-day. It'll get rid o' the mornin', too, quicker 'n any other way. I hain't got anythin' to do but wait the day out till she comes home to-night. She won't be down, I don't suppose, before dark." And Zeph slipped in and sat down humbly in one of the side pews nearest the door, which he knew were free to all. It was early. The bells he had heard were the first bells. No one was in the building except the sexton, who was bustling about, giving last touches of dusting to the pulpit Bible. Presently two women entered, bringing, one a large sheaf of white clematis blooms, the other a high vase filled with the feathery tassels of Indian corn and a few of the graceful, tall, sword-like leaves. It was the custom for the women of this congregation to take turns in decorating the church for the Sunday services; and there was much vying among them, and continual exercise of ingenuity, each to outdo the others in effective arrangement of flowers. As they walked up the aisle Zeph's eyes followed them with astonishment.

"If that ain't just common field corn, 's sure 's I 'm alive," he said; " 'n' it 's prettier 'n the flowers be, heaps! Well, I never!" And for the moment he forgot his misery in watching the women dispose their bouquets on the reading-desk and table.

Presently one of them turned briskly and stepped down the aisle to look up at the desk to see if the arrangement could be improved.

"Oh, Lord!" said Zeph. And in the same instant he buried his face in his hands on the back of the seat in front of him. "That 's that Miss Burr I was askin' after Rushy last night. I don't want her to see me. She 'll be sure to spry round here askin' if I 've found her. She 's dreadful active." And Zeph remained bowed over, his face hid from view, till he heard their steps leaving the church.

It was indeed Miss Sophy; and as she came

down the aisle, her quick eyes catching sight of Zeph's bowed figure, she said to her companion : " Just look at that man all doubled up there in the poor-pews. I do declare, I think it's a shame to have any such thing 's poor-pews : it 's a kind o' badge o' disgrace to sit there; I 've known lots 'n' lots o' poor folks that would n't set foot 'n 'em, not if they never heard a sermon t' their dyin' day, they said. I always feel ashamed when I go by 'em 'n' shut the door t' my pew. It 's borne in on me 't ain't Christian. I think the Catholics are lots better 'n we are about that, — lots. There ain't anything but poor-pews 'n their churches, 'n' that 's the way it ought to be, — free to all."

"How you do talk, Sophy !" replied her companion, good Mrs. Jones. "Why don't you be a Catholic 'n' done with it, if you think their way 's so much better 'n ours ?"

"I don't !" retorted Miss Sophy, — "nothin' o' the kind. But I say they 've got the right

idea about seatin' people. No wonder they
get all the poor people; — I should think they
would. I would n't stir into our church if I
could n't hire my pew, the way 't is now; but 't
ain't right, 'n' 't won't last, neither. You 'll see
it don't last. 'T won't be a great many years
before there 'll be free sittin's, 's they call it,
in every church 'n America."

"Well, then there 'll be lots o' rich people 'll
stay away 'stead o' the poor people!" retorted
Mrs. Jones. "Who wants to sit alongside o'
such a common-looking day-laborer 's that?"
pointing to Zeph.

" He 's clean enough," replied Miss Sophy,
eying Zeph closely as they passed out. " I
would n't mind sitting alongside of him. He
must be awfully broken down, somehow, to be
in here this time o' day, sittin' all scrouched into
a heap like that. I 've a good mind to go speak
to him." And she halted.

" Sophy Burr, you come right straight along

out this minute!" exclaimed Mrs. Jones, raising
her voice indignantly above the decorous whisper in which they had been conversing. "I do
believe you'd take all the dead beats 'n this
town on your shoulders if you could. You
sha'n't go near the man!" And as Miss Sophy,
laughing, allowed herself to be dragged out of
the doorway, Zeph lifted his head with a sense
of relief and escape.

Just as the congregation stood up for the first
singing, the door of the pew where he sat was
timidly opened, and a lame old woman, dressed
in rusty black, leading a little boy, edged shame-
facedly in, glancing with a mute apology in her
eyes at Zeph. Sitting down slowly and with
difficulty, she motioned to the child to stand;
whispering to Zeph, "I've got the rheumatiz
so 't I can't keep on my feet." The child, shy,
and unwonted to the place, refused to stand up,
and clinging to her skirts began to whimper.
Zeph reached out his hand to him, with a smile,

and whispered, "You stand up here by me."
The little fellow yielded at once, the old woman
looking on wonderingly at his sudden obedi-
ence to a stranger. When the singing was over,
the child, instead of drawing close to her, nestled
up to Zeph, and laid one hand confidingly on
his knee. It was a small thing, a very small
thing, but it comforted Zeph. Putting his arm
round the little chap, he drew him closer, and
resting his head comfortably against his shoulder,
whispered, " Go to sleep, sonny, if you want to."
The boy looked up with a vague smile, nestled
again, and shut his eyes. Zeph hugged him
tighter still, stroking his hair, and thinking,
" Poor little fellow! He's got to be a man some
day!"

The minister had risen in the pulpit, opened
the Bible, and was reading his text.

What words were these, falling on Zeph's ear?
No wonder he started, — started so violently
that the child opened his dozing eyes and looked

up in alarm at his new friend. An audible exclamation had nearly burst from Zeph's lips. He gazed at the minister with an emotion very like terror. Was this stranger, this man of whom he had never heard, speaking directly to him, him alone, of all that congregation? Had a message come straight from Heaven to his soul at this crisis in his life? Was it God, and no mere earthly voice, saying these words: " I say not unto thee until seven times, but until seventy times seven "?

"'Seventy times seven!'" repeated the preacher. "We have heard it so often that we do not realize what it means; we set it down as a figure of speech and let it go out of our thoughts. And so it was a figure of speech whereby the Master intended to convey to us the great truth that forgiveness is to last as long as offences last, — unto the very end, no matter how long the life, how bitter the offence. Is not that the way God deals with us? Day after day, year

after year, have we not been offending Him,
breaking His law, slighting His love? We are
old, many of us; have we yet ceased to offend?
Yet here comes this beautiful sun shining on us,
forgiving us anew, this very morning."

"Just what I was thinkin' up on the mesa
there," said Zeph to himself, "only I did n't put
it that way."

"And even if we took the numbers literally,"
the preacher went on, "even then, do we live
up to it? 'Seventy times seven:' four hundred
and ninety. Can we look into our hearts, dealing honestly with ourselves, and say we have forgiven, any one of us,—forgiven so many offences
as that? Friend, neighbor, husband, wife, how
is it? Hast thou been hurt by any one four
hundred and ninety times, and four hundred
and ninety times forgiven the hurt, — forgiven
it, wiped it out?"

It was a homely and realistic putting of the
phrase, but it struck home better than a loftier

one would have done. Not a pew in which
some suddenly remorseful heart, thinking of
some one especial offender, did not own, shame-
smitten, "No, not so many as that;" and no
one more swiftly, remorsefully, than the always
gentle Zeph.

"That 's a fact!" he was saying in his
thoughts. "'T ain't been near so many times 's
that; an' I don't know either 's I 've ever once
really forgiven her, out 'n' out, without layin'
it up to make next time harder; 'n' that ain't
the way the Lord figures it. 'T would go hard
with us ef He did! When Rushy comes home
to-night I don't mean to say 's much 's one
word t' her about anythin', only how glad I
am to get her to home again."

At the end of the sermon the preacher, his
whole soul deeply stirred within him by the
attempt to hold up in its true light, shape,
color, to bring within his people's real grasp
the one eternal talisman,—talisman alike for life

and death, for time and eternity, Forgiveness, —
paused, and with bent head and trembling voice
said, " Shall we dare now to utter the prayer — "
He paused again. " Yes. Since the Master
gave us the words, we must dare to use them;
let us dare now to utter this prayer, ' Forgive us
our trespasses *as* we forgive those who trespass
against us.' "

Sobs were heard throughout the church, and
after the benediction the congregation dispersed
silently, as from a funeral service. There had
indeed been many a grave closed forever in
those last few moments, — closed, and a white
stone set in token; it had been a moment of
inspiration for the preacher, of salvation to the
people.

Zeph passed out of the door, the little boy
still clinging to his hand and the old woman
hobbling by his side. The poor do not stand
on ceremony with each other.

" That was drefful good doctrine he preached,"

she said tremulously, "but 't 's pretty hard to live up to. Guess he hain't had no great crosses hisself."

"I don't know about that," replied Zeph, slowly. "I was a thinkin' mebbe he had had more 'n common, 'r else he would n't ha' thought it all out so clear. 'T seemed to me he felt all he was sayin'."

"There 's things can't be forgiven!" she said sullenly.

Zeph made no reply. Her words grated on him. The child looked up apprehensively as she pulled him away into another road. "I never see him take so to a stranger," she said. "Guess ye 've got children o' your own."

"Yes, two," replied Zeph.

"He 's my grandson," she said. "All I 've got left out o' three boys 'n' two girls : all dead. But there 's lots o' things worse 'n death," she added gloomily. "I 've lived long enough to know that. Good day t' ye." And she turned away.

"'Lots o' things worse 'n death,'" repeated Zeph, as he took his lonely road home. "That's true; 'n' then again 't ain't true. While there 's life, there 's hope." He felt himself strangely cheered and lifted. If forgiveness were so mighty a thing as the preacher had said, — and it must be, since it was all that God had or needed to save the world by, — what more could be needed to straighten out all the tangles of any one little life? He felt his heart full of a larger, better forgiveness towards his wife than he had ever before known; a warmer love than he had felt for many a month.

"There is nothing love cannot do," the preacher had said. "The thing is, to be sure that the love is truly love, and not selfishness."

"I know I love Rushy," thought Zeph, "an' 't ain't selfish love, I know 't ain't! I 'd give

her up to-day, if I could see any way she 'd be
better off without me."

And with his heart full of such thoughts as
these he sat down to wait patiently till night for
her return.

III.

IT was a bitter home-coming,— a bitter return for the forgiving lovingkindness awaiting her.

Tired, more discontented with her home than ever, bearing the baby in her arms, Rushy entered the door, Zephie following, carrying a basket almost heavier than he could lift.

As her eyes fell upon her husband, who went forward to meet her, about to speak words of welcome, she exclaimed testily: " Oh, you 're here, are you ! sittin' round, I s'pose, doin' nothin', ever since I went away."

A hot flush rose in Zeph's face, but he made a mighty effort to curb his anger, and answered gravely : " No, Rushy, I have n't been sittin' much o' the time these last three days. I 've been huntin' you."

"Well, ye might have spared yourself that trouble," she rejoined. "If I'd wanted to be found, I could ha' told ye where I was goin'."

"Rushy," exclaimed Zeph, "don't aggravate me so! I want to live peaceable with ye. I wan't goin' to say a word to ye about havin' been gone all this time; I'll do anythin' on God's earth for ye, Rushy, if ye'll only stay at home 'n' live 's ye'd oughter."

She turned on him like a fury: "Live 's I'd oughter! Ye miserable, mean-spirited, no-'count critter! I've earned six dollars these three days I've been gone; earned it by as hard work 's ever I did in my life, — six dollars in money, besides stuff enough in the basket there to feed the children 'n' me for two days more. Have you been earnin' anything, I'd jest like to know? Have you earned a cent, now, these three days? I say you're the one that had better live as he'd oughter!" And laying the baby on the bed, she began unpacking the basket of food, and with a triumphant air enumerating the articles as she took them out: " There 's cold turkey and veal, and corn-starch, an' a can o' tomatoes, 'n' tea, 'n' coffee, — better vittles than there 's been in this house for one whiles."

Zeph gazed at her in a sort of dumb despair. He had not been prepared for this. Like a strange, far-away sound came into his mind the preacher's words on which he had been musing so much of the day: " There is nothing that love cannot do if it is true love, and not selfishness."

"I got a nice steak for supper," he said. "It 's there on the table."

She glanced at it contemptuously. "What 's two pounds o' steak?" she said. "You can keep it for yourself; we 've got all we want. I 'm goin' down town in the mornin' into rooms I 've got there. I sha'n't live here no longer ! "

"Rooms!" gasped Zeph. "Rushy, what do ye mean? Ye ain't goin' to leave me for good an' all! You don't mean that, Rushy?" And he came towards her with a bound, and putting his hands on her shoulders, looked her in the eyes with an expression which had melted any but a hardened heart. Outraged love, indignation, incredulity, were blended in it; but over and above all, a yearning tenderness, the whole passion of a man's nature, that could not, would not, surrender the loved object.

"I'll never let you go, Rushy, never!" he cried. "Ye don't mean it. You'll never go 'n' shame me 'n' the children 'n' yourself that way. You don't mean it! Say you don't mean it, Rushy!" And his voice broke into almost a sob.

"I do mean it too, Zeph Riker, an' you'll see I mean it. I hate the very sight of you, 'n' you know it; an' if you can't earn a livin', I can, 'n' I'm goin' to; but I ain't goin' to earn it for you too. The rooms is took 'n' paid for, 'n' I 'm goin' into 'em to-morrow."

Zeph buried his face in his hands and was silent. A tempest was raging within him. A terrible impulse to spring upon his wife and kill her swept through his veins, — gone in a second; yet it had been there, and Zeph shuddered as it fled.

Again the far-away refrain sounded in his ears: " There is nothing love cannot do."

" Rushy," he said, "you can't say I hain't made a livin' for us all."

" A livin' ! " she broke in scornfully. " 'T ain't what I call a livin' ! " and she threw a contemptuous glance round the rooms. " A livin' ! " she repeated tauntingly.

" It ain't what it used to be, I know, Rushy," said Zeph. " But that ain't my fault; you stay at home 'n' see to things 's ye used to, 'n' I 'll have everything comfortable for ye mighty quick. I 've been dreadful broke up this last

year, Rushy. You don't keep count o' the days
I 've been goin' round huntin' you; that 's what 's
broke up my work; 'n' then havin' to sell my
tools."

"Yes, I do keep count of 'em, too!" she
shrieked; "you need n't think I don't! An'
every time ye come taggin' on like a fool after
me I hate ye worse; so you can put that 'n
your pipe 'n' smoke it. Perhaps if ye 'd let me
alone 'n' let me come and go like other folks,
without spyin' on me, I should n't ha' gone
away so often. But I 'm goin' now, an' goin' to
stay. This 's the last night ever I 'll sleep 'n
this house; you mark my words!"

"What makes ye say 'like other folks,'
Rushy? You can't fling it up against me that
I hain't tried to shelter ye from gettin' yer name
into folks's mouths. There ain't the livin' man
can say he 's ever heard me open my lips against
ye; nobody 's ever heard it from me that you
was off; many 'n' many 's the time I 've 's

good 's lied to keep it covered up. There
is n't any woman was ever heard of goin' away
from home the way you do, — leastways, no decent woman," he muttered in a bitterer tone.

This last expression seemed to subdue instead of increasing her wrath. She looked at
him for a moment reflectively, as if a new idea
had struck her; then her fury broke forth
anew: "'Decent woman,' eh! Well, I call a decent man, a man that keeps his family comfortable, and can earn good wages, and don't grudge
a woman the price of a bonnet, 'n' 's got some
pride about him 'n' 'll fix up his place, 'n' not
begin a house 'n' then let it stand till the
timbers rots without so much 's roofin' it in.
That 's what I call 'decent;' 'n' I don't call you
anyways decent, 'n' I hain't for a good while,
'n' I don't care who knows it. I 'm done now!
I 've stood it 's long 's I 'm goin' to. I can take
care o' myself 'n' the children, 'n' I will!"

"I hain't ever made any objection to your

earnin' money, Rushy," persisted Zeph, " any way you could do it here 't home."

" How 's anybody to get a thing to do down 'n this Flat? " she replied. " You don't suppose anybody 'd come down here to board? "

"Are you going to take boarders, Rushy? " said Zeph, the words coming slowly from his lips. A new horror was seizing him.

"Yes, I am!" she answered defiantly. "There 's more money in that than anything."

" What 're you goin' to do for furniture? "

" The rooms I 've took is ready furnished," she answered sullenly.

" And the boarders too? " said Zeph, in a hard voice. " I begin to understand. Ye 're goin' in with that Sal Leeson, Rushy."

" Well, supposin' I am!" she muttered. " She 's a good friend to me, 'n' that 's more than any other woman 'n this God-forsaken town 's been! "

"Oh, Rushy, Rushy!" groaned Zeph. "They was all your friends once; everybody liked you when we first come here, you know they did. An' if we was to move away now, 'n' go somewheres else, an' begin over again, ye 'd make plenty o' friends anywheres. Come, Rushy, let's go. I 'll start with ye anywheres ye say; we can sell out for money enough to go with. Come, Rushy!" and he tried to take her hand in his.

She pushed him away roughly, with a brutal laugh. "Zeph Riker," she said, "you 're a fool! Hain't I tried ye? I tell ye I 'm done. I won't never live with ye any more, — never! I 've had my mind made up to that for longer 'n you 've any idea. I 've only been waitin' to see my way clear, 'n' now I see it, 'n' I 'm goin', 'n' you might 's well quit makin' a fuss! I 'm goin'!"

"I forbid ye, Rushy," said Zeph, solemnly. "I forbid ye! I 'm your husband, 'n' I forbid ye."

"Forbid away!" she sneered. "I'm goin' all the same."

Zeph left the house. This was a new pass to which things had come. The tender currents of yearning affection which had been all day setting warmly towards his wife were fast changing under her wicked and cruel words to angry and revengeful feeling. He would talk no more with her. He would go apart by himself and wrestle with this new dilemma. What it was possible for him to do he did not clearly see. Bitterly he wondered within himself what a rich man would do in such a dilemma; if a woman threatening such disgrace to herself and family could be locked up and guarded like a lunatic; what provision the law made for such contingencies.

"It's easy enough for the judge to say, if 't came into court, that she's got to stay 't home; but that won't keep her there, 'n' locks 'n' bars would n't either, if she's made up her mind to go; 'n' I can't stay at home 'n' watch her, nor pay anybody else for doin' it either. Lord have mercy on me, now! I don't see any way to turn." And half blinded by these whirling, miserable thoughts, Zeph went on walking, walking, he knew not where. At last he turned.

"I'll go home," he said. "She sha'n't have it to say I didn't stay with her to-night. Perhaps I can bring her round yet."

But when he entered the house his first glance showed him that she had not faltered in her intention, and that the morning would see it carried out. Two boxes stood in the middle of the kitchen floor locked and corded. Her own clothes and the children's had all been taken out of the closet and drawers. The steak lay untouched on the platter where he had left it. The basket of provisions she had brought from the camp was repacked, and a brown paper tied tight over its top. "She don't even mean to get breakfast here," thought Zeph, as he passed through into the bedroom. The children were in their bed asleep, undressed as usual. Rushy lay on the outside of the bed, none of her clothes removed, her arm flung over the little ones with an expression of fierce protection, which smote Zeph none the less because he could not have analyzed the feeling.

"She need n't ha' thought I 'd take 'em away from her in their sleep," he thought. "What could I do with the baby, anyway, even if I was minded to steal 'em from her?"

Rushy was asleep and breathing heavily. She had indeed worked hard and was tired out. As Zeph stood looking down on her face there swept over him a storm of memories of the early days of their acquaintance, courtship, and marriage, — days when he was like a man treading in air, so foolish and fond was he; so blind to everything except her beauty and her fascinating, bewitching ways. Every reminiscence of these was now but fuel to the fires that were consuming him.

"There does n't anybody know any better 'n I do," he said, in jealous anguish, "what ways she's got o' takin' a man off his feet. I don't blame any of 'em, not a mite, I don't, if she makes up her mind to fool 'em. There was n't ever the man born could stand out against her!" and he groaned.

The sound awoke Rushy. Looking up at him angrily, she exclaimed, "Keep away, can't ye? Let me alone!"

"I was n't going to touch ye, Rushy," said Zeph; and he crossed the room and threw himself, without undressing, on the outside of the bed.

Slowly the night wore away, Rushy sleeping heavily, as undisturbed as if no tragedy brooded over her home; Zeph lying motionless, with wide-open eyes, asking himself over and over and over again the bootless question, what he should do. It was like a waking nightmare, the sense of near catastrophe which weighed on his helplessness.

Once in the night the baby woke and cried hoarsely. Rushy rose, lighted the lamp, and attended lovingly to the little creature's wants. As she was doing so she met Zeph's steady gaze following her every motion. Her face hardened instantly into an evil and defiant expression which cut Zeph to the quick.

"She hates me," he thought. "That wa'n't anythin' less than hate, that look she had then." He was glad when she blew out the light, and without speaking threw herself again on the bed.

The bedroom windows faced the east. At the first ray of light Rushy sprang up, and rousing the children began dressing them. Zeph sat on the edge of his bed, watching her silently. He had resolved not to speak first, to simply bide the issue as she might force it upon him. His continued silence made her uneasy. From time to time she glanced at him apprehensively. His quiet, calm look made her anxious. She was not clear in her own mind what it meant, nor what might be the extent of his power in the matter. The evil counsellors with whom she had resolved to now cast in her fortunes had warned her that the law would uphold her husband in compelling her to remain at home, or in taking the children from her did he choose to let her go.

"Let him just try it!" she had answered boastfully. "I'd like to see any man take my children away from me."

"But it's the law, Rushy," Nat Leeson had said. To tell the truth, infatuated as he was with Rushy, he was by no means unwilling that the children should be left with their father.

"I don't care if it's a hundred laws," Rushy had made answer. "I tell you nobody's goin' to get my children away from me. I'll make a good livin' for 'em, 'n' no judge is goin' to take 'em away 'n' give 'em to Zeph Riker to take care of! I ain't a mite afraid."

But she was; and the longer Zeph's silence lasted, and the more glances she stole at his calm, resolute face, the more afraid she grew; and it was with an almost sinking heart that at last, when she had no longer any excuse for further delay, she turned to him and said, with a poor attempt at bravado in her tone, "I'm going now, Zeph." She was tying her bonnet-strings as she spoke. Her hands trembled. Zeph saw it.

"Have n't ye thought better o' what ye said last night, Rushy?" he asked.

The gentleness of his voice and manner deceived her. It is a piteous thing to see how, in this life, the gentler and finer organized nature is always the one to suffer most and come off vanquished in collisions, and the coarse-grained, brutal one to triumph.

"No, I hain't!" she cried in a harsh tone. "I've thought better 'n' better of goin'. Ye poor shiftless thing, ye, I donno 's ye've got spirit enough to take care o' yourself, let alone taking care of a wife an' children!"

"Ye know ye're sayin' what's not true, Rushy," said Zeph, gravely, with no excitement in his manner. "Ye're only trumpin' up things like that to say to folks to keep 'em from shamin' ye 's ye deserve. Ye know you've had a good home with me, 'n' a man to love ye 's nobody else ever'll love ye, out o' all these that's been foolin' 'n' tollin' ye to the devil."

"You go to the devil yourself then," cried Rushy, "'n' don't sit there talkin' to me like a preacher. Look to home! If I was a mind to cast up at you, I could do it fast enough; but I've got too much to do. Come, Zephie, come with mam! You've got to carry the basket, but 't ain't so heavy 's 't was last night. There'll

7

be a man here to get the things this noon," she added, turning again to Zeph.

He did not heed her. He was gazing at little Zephie. The child stood looking from his mother to his father, the tears slowly rolling down his cheeks. He was only ten years old, but he understood too well the wretched, shameful scene. It was not the first he had witnessed.

"Come on, Zephie," said his mother, moving towards the door. The boy did not stir.

Zeph held out his hands to him. "Stay here with pappy," he said. "Mam 'll come back perhaps sooner 'n she says. You stay with pappy." And tears which all Rushy's cruelty had failed to wring from Zeph's eyes fell now as he drew his boy close and folded him in his arms.

Rushy halted. She was undecided. "Oh, well," she said, in a hard tone, affecting to laugh, "Zephie can stay with you if he wants to; he 'll be glad enough to come to his mammy, though, when he 's hungry. He knows where

't is. When you want some o' mam's gingerbread, Zephie, you come down and get it."
And without another look at her husband she
left the house, the baby in her arms.

For some moments Zeph sat like one
stunned. He had not really believed she would
do it; or that it would be anything more than
her previous absences. But he realized now
that it was different; something had passed,
had gone forever; a new gulf had opened between him and his wife. He was recalled to
himself by little Zephie, who still stood between his knees, softly crying.

"What makes mam go away?" he sobbed.

The innocent question unnerved Zeph. He
too sobbed, and holding the child convulsively
to his breast, cried: "I don't know, Zephie;
something dreadful 's got into mam. Pappy's
afraid she 's crazy; but perhaps she 'll come
back different."

"She won't ever come back, — not into this

house," said the boy. " I heard her tell Sal so last night."

" What did Sal say? " asked Zeph.

" She said she 'd be just fool enough !" he replied.

So these were the influences under which Rushy had been. He knew it before, but the child's artless story seemed to vivify his realization of it.

" What did mam say when Sal said that?" asked Zeph.

" I don't know," said the child; " I did n't hear her say anything. Nat said —"

" What did Nat say? " broke in Zeph, so fiercely that the child started.

" Nat said she 'd have to come back."

" He did, did he? " muttered Zeph.

" Zephie," he continued, " you an' pappy 'll live together now till mam comes home. We 'll have some beefsteak now for breakfast, 'n' then pappy 'll take you over to Gammer's to stay

while he goes to work; 'n' you can go to school
with Bud; 'n' to-night pappy 'll get a nice
supper."

"Will you have gingerbread?" asked Zephie.

"Yes," replied the father, "gingerbread and
apples." And by some inexplicable mental pro-
cess the very incongruity between this question and answer and the depth of misery in his
breast moved him to laughter, and helped him
as no other thing just at that moment could
have done.

Gammer Stein was "Gammer" to the whole
neighborhood. Not a family in all the Flat,
or, as Gammer's Missourian tongue called it,
"Flairt," but went to her for sympathy, coun-
sel, help, in the perplexities and troubles of
their hard-working lives. She was the only
person with whom Zeph had ever talked of his
troubles with his wife. A great-hearted, tireless, motherly woman, caring tenderly, through
all her poverty, for every one, neighbor or

stranger, poorer than herself; bringing up, in her old age, with the affectionate patience of a mother, two orphan grandchildren; bearing with more than wifely, almost with superhuman, good-nature the ill-temper of a brutal husband, to whom even his seventy years had brought neither decency nor moderation of passions, — Gammer Stein was one of those unknown, unnoted saints, whose lives, unwritten in words, are written in records of influence as ineffaceable, as eternal, as the records of changes and influences in the solid substance of the earth.

It was not a year after she arrived in town, with the two little grandsons clinging to her skirts, and calling loudly, unceasingly, from morning till night, "Gammer, Gammer!" before the whole neighborhood where she lived had learned to echo the children's name and the children's cry; and it had so nearly passed out of the memory of the place that the old woman

had another name than "Gammer," that when, as
sometimes happened, a stranger asked her real
name, the people had to bethink themselves, to
recall that "Mary," and not " Gammer," was the
name by which she had been christened.

Two weeks had passed since Rushy bade her
defiant farewell to her husband. It was again
a cloudless summer Sabbath morning, and the
hush of the beneficent rest it had brought
brooded over all the working-people's homes
in the Flat. Even the belated curls of smoke
seemed to ascend lingeringly, as if knowing
that on this day there was no hurry about anything. But there was no curl of smoke going
up out of the chimney of Zeph's house. More
than once Gammer Stein had glanced that way
in neighborly curiosity, and had thought to
herself, " Poor fellow! he sleeps late to-day.
It's well he can."

As the morning wore on, and still no sign
of life came from the house, her thoughts took

a shape of anxiety, and she said to her husband, "I allow Zeph's sick. He hain't stirred yit. Yeow jest go over 'n' see ef he wants anythin'."

"I allow he kin run his sickness hisself," growled Wilhelm, who was the antipodes of his wife in every one of the traits which so endeared her to her neighbors. "I allow I hain't got no call to go aout nussin' jest yit. Yeow kin ef yer want ter. I allow yer fool enough."

Gammer glanced at him reproachfully. For fifty years she had held her peace at such replies as this; but this morning, for some reason, her mild soul was moved to make answer. "Ef yer wuz layin' sick in yer bed hyar, 'n' nobody ter come nigh yer, I allow Zeph 'd be ther fust one as 'ud be lookin' arter yer; I allow he would. He's all alone thar. The boy's ben these two days daown 't his mother's. I seed 't was cuttin' inter Zeph, the little feller's goin' off ter her. I wouldn't wonder a mite ef

Zeph hed gone killed hisself. He's sed more
'n once he bleeved she'd drive him t' it; 'n' I
see him sharpenin' a big knife 'n aour grind-
stone. Thet wuz last Wednesday; no, 't wuz
Toosday. I wuz ironin', 'n' sez I, jest careless,
'What yer sharpenin' 't so sharp fur, Zeph?'
'n' he sez, sez he, 'I ain't gwine ter cut my
throat, Gammer, yit, never yeow be afeerd;'
jest 's ef he seen I wuz thinkin'; 'n' I sez ter
him, 'Naow, Zeph, ef yeow 've hed a hell 'n
this life, yeow don't want ter go right straight
inter anuther wuss one, dew yer? An' I
allow ef yer go 'n' murder yeourself, ye 'll jest
go right straight inter torment thar won't be
no gettin' shet of, never!' I jest spoke plain
ter him."

"I sh'd think ser," growled Wilhelm; "allers
a meddlin' in business 't ain't any o' yeourn. I
allow 't ain't nothin' ter yeow ef Zeph Riker
cuts his throat ef he wants ter."

"I allow 't is," continued Gammer, placidly;

" I allow he 's my brother, accordin' to Scriptur'; thar ain't nobody gwine to kill hisself thet I knows on, ef I kin hender him."

The words had hardly passed her lips, when a sharp cry, " Gammer, Gammer! " came from the front of the house. Both Gammer and Wilhelm sprang to their feet.

" That 's Zephie," exclaimed Gammer, as she ran to the door. Little Zephie was running by at the top of his speed. As he passed, he shrieked, " Nat 's cut pappy all ter pieces ! He 's bleedin'! The men 's bringin' him."

Horror-stricken, Gammer followed the child, and overtook him as he was vainly trying with his trembling little fingers to fit the key into the door.

" Oh, hurry, hurry ! " he cried. " Oh, Gammer, get the door open ! Pappy told me to run 'n' git his bed ready."

" He 's alive, then ? " gasped Gammer.

" Yes, he 's alive," sobbed Zephie, " but he 's

bleedin'; his face's all cut. Oh, Gammer, Gammer, when I'm a man I'll kill Nat!"

"Hush, child! naow don't yeow talk thet way; tew killin's is wuss 'n one! It's all murder," said Gammer, moving about the rooms distractedly, hardly knowing what she did, as she heard the steady tramp of men's feet nearing the house.

It was a ghastly burden they brought, a ghastly story they had to tell. After they had made the wounded man as comfortable as it was possible to make him with the scanty accommodations at hand, the doctor drew Gammer aside and told her the tale.

It seemed that Zeph, poor fellow, had not been able to keep away from the house where his wife was living. Not only did he yearn for the sight of her face and the baby's, but he had a foolish notion that his being occasionally seen there would be a shelter to her reputation. He had even said, with incredible magnanimity, to

Sal Leeson, who reluctantly bore that much of testimony to his goodness, " It's all against my will, Rushy 's bein' here; but so long 's she's my wife, 'n' 's got my children along with her, it's better for all round that I should be here some o' the time, whether she wants me or not!"

The evil-doers, men and women, who consorted in the place, had been more than once shamed and sobered and finally driven out of Rushy's room by the sight of the silent, sad-faced man whose name she had so dishonored. It was incredible that he could have borne it. But he did; and it had become evident that if Rushy was insensible to his presence, others were not, and a new feeling of respect and sympathy for Zeph had arisen, even in the minds of those previously most hostile to him. Nat himself had been sometimes shamed into withdrawing from the stern, silent gaze of the injured husband. Encouraged by these signs

that the man was not wholly insensible to disgrace, Zeph had resolved to make one effort to
reason with him, and had timed this remon-
strance unluckily, addressing him when he was
sufficiently under the influence of liquor to be
savagely irritable. It was late on Saturday
evening. As Nat entered Rushy's kitchen with
the easy familiarity of one privileged, Zeph,
who had been waiting for him to come in, rose,
and said, " Nat, I owe all my troubles with my
wife to you. If it was n't for you — "

He did not finish the sentence. Seizing a
carving-knife which lay on the table, Nat sprang
on him like a tiger. Zeph, wholly unarmed,
caught up a chair to ward off the blows, and one
swift, terrible second saw the two men wrestling
in a life-and-death fight. Stretched from one
corner to the other of the room was a line on
which Rushy had towels and small articles hung
airing after the wash. The chair with which
Zeph was hitting out blindly caught in this

line, throwing him to the floor; and that was the last he knew till, coming vaguely to his senses, he heard voices above him: one, his wife's, angry, hard, — how it smote him! — "I tell you he sha'n't stay here! I've left him! I won't have him laid on that bed! He's no business here, any way!"

Zeph opened his eyes. Opposite him was Nat, raging, swearing, held firm by two policemen, who were dragging him out of the room.

"Why did n't ye let me alone till I'd finished my job?" he bellowed, like a wild beast in his fury, Rushy, one hand on his arm, one on his mouth, vainly striving to check him from incriminating himself further.

Zeph closed his eyes at the harrowing sight. Yes; why had they not let Nat finish his job! How much better it would have been! What a release from misery!

Then he heard a voice saying angrily to

Rushy, — it was the doctor, — " I don't care
who he is or what he is, he has got to be laid
on that bed, I tell you ! Are you a woman, or
a devil? Stand out of the way ! " And then
Zeph felt himself lifted and borne, and a buzz
of murmuring voices, and sharp stinging pains
in his cheek and throat; and then he sank away
and knew no more until in the night, when he
waked again to himself, and all was still, no
sound except the loud ticking of a clock; and
some man sitting by him, a stranger, said in a
not unkind voice, " Hey! 'wake, are ye? Want
anything?" and Zeph had said feebly, " Water,"
and had tried to ask for Rushy, but the words
would not form themselves; and while he was
struggling to speak them, he floated off, he
thought, on a big white cloud, and the air was
full of the sound of bells ringing, and he remembered that it must be Sunday, and opened his
eyes again, and saw the broad daylight stream-
ing into the room, and the doctor standing in

the doorway, and men's heads rising one behind the other, and the doctor's voice again, angry and indignant, reasoning with Rushy. Could those tones be Rushy's, and those cruel words? Yes, it was Rushy, saying in a shrill voice, " I don't care! I tell ye I won't have him here. He's brought me trouble enough a'ready; an' now he's got Nat into prison, 'n' I don't care what becomes of him. 'T was all his fault. He begun the fight, aggravatin' Nat. Nat never spoke the first word."

And above all the confused and struggling sounds of the excited voices still pealed on the church-bells; and at the sound Zeph's brain seemed suddenly to clear itself, and strength to come back to him; and half raising himself in the bed, he spoke aloud: " Say, doctor, let them carry me home; I'd rather go. 'T 'won't hurt me. I ain't very bad hurt, am I?"

A hush fell on the group of excited talkers. They had thought him asleep.

"No, you're not very bad hurt," said the doctor, coming to the bedside and feeling his pulse. "I don't suppose it'll do you any hurt to be carried over to your house. But you've got an ugly cut in your face, came mighty near being your throat, and it'll need watching for a few days, two weeks maybe. You've got to be tended pretty close. You can't be left all alone in the house." And the doctor glanced wrathfully at Rushy, who stood silent, sullen, looking down on the floor.

"I'll manage that, doctor," said Zeph, cheerfully, "if you'll just get me home. My boy'll go with me, I guess; he's there 'most o' the time. I'll have to keep him out of school a few days, but after that I'll do for myself. I've got good neighbors out there."

All this time Rushy spoke no word, but her face grew harder and darker with every syllable that fell from her husband's lips. She saw how his words were telling against her. Even her evil

8

comrade, Sal Leeson, bent almost compassion-
ately over the bed and wiped Zeph's forehead
as he spoke.

"I say, Rushy," she muttered, "you might
let him stay just a few days; I'll look after
him."

Before Rushy could reply, Zeph cried out,
"No, no! I tell you I won't stay. Doctor,
it 'ud kill me to stay," he continued pleadingly. "Oh, get me out o' here 's quick 's
you can!"

They were all rough men who were standing
there ready to give what help might be in their
power, but there was not a man among them
whose pulses did not beat quicker at this cry
of Zeph's. They lifted him in their arms tenderly, as if he had been a helpless woman,
and many a resentful glance was shot back
at the unfeeling wife, who neither moved nor
spoke as her husband was borne out of the
house.

"Good-by, Rushy," he said. "I'm awful sorry to have got ye into this trouble. But ye know 't wan't any o' my doin', Rushy. Ye know 't wan't. Say good-by to me, Rushy. P'raps I'll never see ye again."

"Good-by," she said sullenly, without looking up. In league and fast bound with malignant spirits, surely, must Rushy Riker's heart have been, to have resisted the appeal of that moment. Even Sal Leeson was crying; but Rushy's eyes glittered hard and dry with an evil light. Her guilty and passionate heart was full of terror for Nat. She had overheard one of the policemen say, as they dragged him off after the fray, "You'll swing for this night's work, Nat Leeson;" and Nat, frantic in his fury, had replied, "Swing and be damned! If you'd let me alone a minute longer, I'd have finished him!"

Rushy knew only too well that if Zeph was to die of his hurts, these reckless words of Nat's would carry terrible weight against him in the trial for murder which must follow. Her whole nature was on fire with apprehensions, wild and bootless plottings and plannings, and over and above all raged an unreasoning anger against her husband for having been the occasion of such danger to Nat.

"If worst comes to worst, I'll swear him out myself," said the wretched woman. "I'll swear Zeph set on him with the knife first. 'T was just the same 's a knife, the words he used. They just made Nat crazy."

The jail was in full sight from her door: a square, stone building with grated windows, at the back a high fence surrounding an enclosure in which a man had been hung only a few months previous, — hung for a murder committed in a sudden fray not unlike this one between her husband and Nat. As Rushy recalled the day of this hanging and the crowd of men and women she had seen outside the

fence eagerly striving, like wild beasts athirst
for blood, to look through cracks in the fence,
to climb up and see over, her heart sickened
within her; clenching her fist, she shook it
toward the jail and muttered: "They sha'n't
ever hang Nat. I'll burn the place down over
their heads first. If 't is stone I'll fire it somehow, or I'll get him poison! They sha'n't
hang him!"

The church in which Zeph had listened two
weeks before to the sermon on forgiveness
stood only a few rods from Rushy's house. As
the men were carrying him past the door the
choir had just begun the singing of the first
hymn.

"Stop a minute, can't ye?" whispered Zeph.
"It jars me awful, bein' carried; just rest a
minute here 'n this shade." He would not
confess that it was for sake of the singing that
he wished to stop. With closed eyes he lay
listening. He could not hear the words, but

the tune was one of the sweet old-fashioned ones he had heard sung when he was a child; and there were words echoing in his thoughts which seemed to fit strangely into its rhythm, — words echoing yet in the air, though it was now fourteen days since their syllables had been spoken: " Yea, I say unto you, until seventy times seven."

" I don't know what's got into me," thought Zeph, " to be so haunted like by them words. I don't lay no claim to bein' a Christian, 'n' I'd just as soon kill that Nat this minute 's I would a pizen snake; but I can't get free from them words."

IV.

DURING these two weeks which had brought such tragedy into Zeph's life the memory of him and his troubles had by no means died out of Miss Sophy's mind. She found herself reverting with strange persistency to the trains of unwonted thought awakened within her by his inexplicable devotion to his unworthy wife. The more she thought, the surer she became that the man had done only what she herself would have done in similar circumstances. "'For better, for worse,'" she repeated. "That does n't mean but one thing; there are n't any two ways o' readin' or sayin' such plain words as that! An' it 's 'worse' he 's got, no mistake. But I 'm as sure 's I 'm alive, that there ain't many men would take it the way he does; it 's more the way a woman 'ud do. Strange, too; such a great strong man 's he is! six foot if he 's an inch, — I 'd have thought he 'd made short work o' any man that came foolin' round his wife. I 'll go up 'n' see how he 's gettin' along to-morrow."

But times were busy with Miss Sophy. Midsummer brought crowds of travellers to Pendar Basin, and the reputation of Miss Sophy's good table was so wide that her doors were besieged with applicants for board. She had to turn them away by dozens, much to the distress of her thrifty soul; but, as she curtly remarked sometimes to those who wearied her by importunities, "Four walls is four walls, 'n' ye can't make 'em any bigger. It 's more for my interest to take ye than 't is for yours to come, but I have n't got so much as room for a shake-down left; that 's the truth."

In addition to this inroad of boarders, Miss Sophy had other perplexities on her mind; one

of her wise and long-seeing measures had been
the purchase of a small ranch, a few miles
from town, where she raised vegetables and
kept poultry and cows. Until this summer the
scheme had worked well; the ranch, in the
hands of a faithful Swede and his wife, yielding
her a profit on the investment, and contributing
no small share to the fame of her house. She
had called the ranch " Greenhills," partly in
affection for her old Vermont home, partly because the house stood in a little park-like open,
surrounded by low hills which had springs in
them, and were consequently green when the
rest of the plains around were sere and brown.
Greenhills butter and Greenhills poultry, whenever there was any surplus above Miss Sophy's
own needs, brought fancy prices in market; and
the sole air-castle Miss Sophy had, was the
vision of the time when she would have money
enough put away in the bank and on loans to
make it safe for her to give up keeping boarders

and live at Greenhills. And it was Greenhills
she had in her thoughts on that evening when
Zeph knocked at her kitchen door, and she had
with a hasty impulse, so unlike her usual cir-
cumspection, told him she could give him work.
Something in Zeph's eyes inspired her with sudden and entire confidence in him, and she would
then and there have taken him into her employ,
had he been so minded; she was near at her
wits' end with the miserable and dishonest fel-
lows she had employed on the place since the
Swede had gone away in the spring. Bitten
by the mining craze, of which there had been a
fresh outburst in the region, he had left her,
with only a week's warning, in the midst of the
spring planting, and everything had seemed to
be going from bad to worse ever since.

"If I could just get that Zeph up there to
overlook things! I believe he 's as honest 's a
Newfoundland dog," said Miss Sophy. And it
was, after all, not wholly philanthropy which

made her, on the very Sunday afternoon after
Zeph's fray with Nat, turn her steps once more
towards his house. With her usual straightfor-
wardness she was going directly to him to offer
him the situation. " An' if that wife o' his is in
the house," said the resolute Miss Sophy, " I
sha'n't mince any words with her. I shall just
tell her it 's her husband I want, an' not her,
'n' she won't be allowed to set her foot on the
place. If he 's fool enough to come home to
her Sundays he can." From which it is plain
to be seen, that, spite of her tender meditations
on the solemn words of the marriage service,
and on the touching faithfulness of Zeph to his
erring wife, Miss Sophy was not quite sound in
the practical application of the doctrine.

But Providence intervened to save her the
shock of being suddenly confronted by the spec-
tacle of the wounded, helpless Zeph. As she
crossed the open in front of his house, Gammer
Stein's sharp eyes spied her. Gammer was

keeping the Sabbath in her wonted fashion, by taking in vigorous hand the bodies of her grandchildren. Cleanliness, in her creed, took place of all especial observance of conventional godliness on the seventh day; and a terrible day it made of it for Bud and Tim. No possible Sunday purgatory of hard benches and long sermons, as experienced by the children of more Orthodox parents, could have compared in terror with the Sunday scrubbings and combings to Gammer Stein's grandchildren. The foreshadowing gloom of it fell on them of a Saturday, and the smart and tingle of it lasted all day Monday, and longer.

It was at a lucky crisis for Bud that Miss Sophy appeared on the scene. The six days' tangle of his hair had proved too much both for his grandmother's patience and his own, and he had just broken into loud crying, and she into something as near scolding as her placid nature ever reached, when, suddenly throwing combs, brushes, scissors, all to the floor, the old lady cried, "Thar she goes now! Wall, ef thet ain't cur'us!" And without another word she ran out of the house, waving her arms and calling aloud: "Hyar! Miss Burr! Yeow hyar! Don't yer go nigh ther house. Yeow wait tell I kin come up ter ye."

Miss Sophy, surprised, and, if the truth were told, not wholly pleased, stood still, as admonished, till Gammer reached her, and then coolly waited for her to speak. Nothing daunted, Gammer gasped breathlessly, "I allowed ye wuz gwine ter Zeph's, wan't yer?"

"Yes," replied Miss Sophy.

"Wall, I allowed ye wuz, 'n' I jest dropped everythin'. I wuz er grapplin' wi' Bud's hair; it's somethin' orful, Bud's hair ez: 'n' I jest throwed the combs daown 'n' run ter tell yer not ter go nigh ther haouse." And Gammer stopped for want of breath.

"Why not?" exclaimed Miss Sophy, curiosity

getting the better of her reserve. "What's happened? Who's sick?"

"'T ain't no sickness, it's wuss!" replied Gammer, sententiously. "It 's wuss 'n any sickness. Thet Nat's cut Zeph all ter pieces, 'n' he 's layin' thar; the doctor 's in thar naow,—the city doctor; pore folks hez ter hev him, yer know. I allow he don't know much; Zeph wuz bleedin' orful when they brung him over; I wuz thar. I never seed sech a sight, 'n' I don't never want ter. I allow he 'll die, sure."

"Cut to pieces!" interrupted Miss Sophy. "What do you mean? He can't be cut to pieces! Is she in there? Did he find her? Who 's takin' care o' him?"

"Well, it ez in his face 'n' jaw, mostly," replied Gammer; "he ain't cut nowhar 's else; 'n' ther doctor sez when his beard 's growed out agen full, 't won't show none. The doctor, he allowed ez he would n't ha' hed sech a cut 's

thet not fur no woman livin'; he allowed he
would n't."

It was of no use to attempt to direct courses
and channels of narrative in Gammer Stein's
mouth; once launched, she was as unmanage-
able as a rudderless boat, and veered wildly
from past to present, from actual to hypotheti-
cal, from descriptive to didactic, according to
the quarter from which each sudden reminiscence and emotion struck her. After one or
two vain attempts to interpolate questions or
get some consecutive order of statement, Miss
Sophy abandoned all such efforts and patiently listened, and in the course of half an
hour was in possession of the substantial facts
of the case.

Two scarlet spots glowed on her cheeks. "It
is the most shameful thing I ever heard!" she
cried, when at length Gammer paused.

"Ain't it?" said Gammer. "Ain't she jest
a disgrace ter ther whole on us? I allow thar

ain't no hell, wharever 't is ner whatsomeever it's made outer, thet's bad enough fur sech 's her."

" I'm goin' in to see him," said Miss Sophy, firmly.

" Yer ain't, though, be yer?" said Gammer. " Be yer reel steady headed? He looks orful."

" I'm goin' in," repeated Miss Sophy. " He's got to be looked after. I shall ask the doctor what he ought to have to eat."

" I allow I'll go 'long tew," said Gammer. " Tew's better 'n one." And she accompanied Miss Sophy to the door. As they reached it, the doctor came out.

" Ah! Ah, Miss Burr," he said, in a tone of relief, " I'm glad to see you here. How did you hear of it? The man is badly hurt, but he will pull through if he can be kept quiet. He wants nursing, though."

Miss Sophy nodded. " Yes, I should think

he did," she said in a wrathful tone. " I suppose that good-for-nothing wife of his — "

" Don't speak of her ! " broke in the doctor.
" She 's a regular she-devil ! If she shows her
face here, I 'll have her arrested. He 's better
alone, than with her round. She won't come,
anyhow ; she 's left him."

" Humph ! " said Miss Sophy, with something
between a snort and a sob. " Good riddance !
I should say."

" The little chap 's very handy," continued the
doctor, " and he seems fond of his father. I 've
showed him how to keep the bandages wet ;
he must n't swallow anything but liquids for a
good many days, — only milk at first. In a day
or two, if you can give him some of your good
soups, Miss Burr, that will be all he will need.
He 'll pull through. It is a close shave ; but the
man 's got the constitution of an ox."

" I 'll see he has the soups, doctor," said Miss
Sophy, turning away.

" Ain't yer gwine in?" cried Gammer, disap-
pointed. " Yer said ye wuz gwine in. I allow 't
w'ud be good fur him ter know he 'd got some
friends more 'n he 'd knowed on."

Miss Sophy hesitated. A sudden repugnance
had seized her.

" No," she said, " not to-day. I 'll be up
again to-morrow. You can tell him I was here,
and that I 'll look after him. He need n't give
himself one mite of uneasiness about food. I 'll
see that he 'n' the boy have all they need.
I 'll look after 'em."

" Then I allaow they 'll be looked arter," said
Gammer. " Anybody 'd know jest by ther
way yer step aout yer hed n't no slouch abaout
yeow! Yer powerful active, yer air, fur a
woman er yeour build. It's cur'us naow what
tuk Zeph ter yeour door thet night, ain't it?
He hain't hed much luck, but thet wuz luck; I
allow ter yeou, looks like 't wuz! Good day t'
ye, good day! I allaow thet Bud 's got hes

hair inter a wuss snarl 'n 't wuz afore, while
we 've been talkin'. Ez soon 's I 've got through
cleanin' him up I shell go inter Zeph's 'n'
straighten aout things thar."

Miss Sophy went home like one walking in a
dream of horror. In the whole course of her
placid thirty-five years no such glimpse as this
of the dark side of human life and human
nature had ever reached her. The currents of
existence in her native village were always as
smooth as they were dull; no crime had ever
been committed there, neither did any of the
great daily newspapers come into the place
with its record of the wretched iniquities of
the outside world. Vaguely Miss Sophy knew
that such things were, as she knew that there
were volcanic eruptions and cyclones; but to
find herself thus face to face with, in fact almost
involved in, one of the most dreadful of all
human tragedies, stunned her.

"Right here in Pendar Basin, too," she said

to herself, " in this little village, and 'mongst workin' folks, too; I declare it's awful! I don't like bein' mixed up in it, anyhow. It don't seem decent to even know about it. But somebody 's got to look after that man, that 's certain; 'n' I 'd rather do it myself without any help than go 'n' tell anybody such a story 's that. I 'd bite my tongue off first."

And so with a grim repression which cost Miss Sophy a dear expenditure of nerve force in the self-restraint it involved, she went about her business and said not a word to any one of her ministrations to the wounded man. It was not till the fourth day that she nerved herself up to accompany Gammer to his bedside. The sight overcame her, and routed her last vestige of cowardly unwillingness to an open responsibility about the case.

" I don't care what 's to be said," she exclaimed, " nor who 's mixed up in it; that man ain't goin' to lie another day in that hole. I 'm

goin' to have him moved right out to Greenhills and taken care of decent. I can drive
out there every day 'n' see to him. I do go
out pretty near every day 's 't is; 'n' the air out
there 'll half cure him. Why, the flies 'n that
room o' his are enough to kill him,—just the
flies alone! There ain't a window nor a door
out to Greenhills that has n't got mosquito net
in it."

"Yer don't mean it, dew yer?" exclaimed
Gammer Stein, taken all aback at the sug-
gestion.

"I do, too!" cried Miss Sophy. "I 'm going
to the doctor this minute to ask him if he 's got
anything to say against it."

"I dunno 's Zeph ud be willin'," began Gammer, hesitatingly. "I allow—"

"He 'll go if I come for him," interrupted
Miss Sophy, impatiently. "He is n't a fool,—
that is, not in everything," she added testily.
"I want him out there to work 's soon 's he 's

able, 'n' he 'll be right there to begin." And Miss Sophy was off.

In an hour she was back again with the doctor, who was heartily in favor of her scheme. In fact, he said the man's one chance for life lay in some such change; the wounds were not of themselves enough to kill him, but the solitary brooding over his troubles was keeping up a fever in which he grew daily weaker and daily worse.

When Miss Sophy's plan was explained to Zeph, he lifted his eyes to her face in a long, scrutinizing gaze.

" I donno what reason ye 've got, ma'am," he said slowly, " for takin' so much trouble for me. I ain't worth it."

" I dare say you ain't," replied Miss Sophy, " but you can't be left to die here o' these flies. If there was a hospital, that 's the place you ought to go to ; but there ain't any, 'n' my house out to Greenhills's plenty o' room in it,

'n' there 's a man out there can see to all you
want. You don't want anythin', the doctor
says, but good food 'n' to be quiet; 'n' you can
have that out there without its costin' anybody
anythin', so we 've decided to move you out
there. The men 'll be here about four o'clock
with the wagon."

"Greenhills ranch?" said Zeph, inquiringly,
— a faint gleam of interest lighting up the sad-
ness in his eyes.

"Yes," said Miss Sophy, "that 's my ranch;
that 's where I was going to give you work,
if you 'd wanted it, that night you came to my
house ; 'n' just 's soon 's you 're on your feet
there 's plenty for you to do out there."

Zeph made no reply. His eyes turned to
Zephie, who stood at the foot of the bed,
listening wide-mouthed to the startling proposition.

Miss Sophy misunderstood the expression of
Zeph's gaze.

"Yes, the boy can go too," she said. " It 'll be handy to have him there. There 's plenty o' room."

" I was a thinkin' that it would be hard to be where I could n't see him, ma'am," said Zeph, slowly. "But I could n't take him out there. He 'd have to stay with his mother."

" Stay with his mother ! " shrieked Miss Sophy; and, " His mother ! " cried the doctor. "What d' ye mean, man ! "

Zeph's face flushed. " I 've been talkin' a good many things over with the boy," he said, " an' he 'd rather stay an' help his mother, — a while, at any rate, till we see how things goes. He was goin' to see her to-day. That 's all settled, sir," he added, as the doctor opened his lips again with an impatient ejaculation. " There 's things that nobody knows anything about except folks themselves, an' other folks can't judge. I had been plannin' to go away for a spell 's soon 's I was fit to work, 'n'

Zephie was to stay with his mother till I come back."

There was a dignity in Zeph's tone and bearing which lifted the homely language to the level of eloquence; and the earnest answering look on the child's face, as he met his father's eyes, completed the revelation. This was indeed no matter for "other folks" to judge of or to interfere with.

"I'll go out to your place, ma'am," continued Zeph, again fixing a bewildered and scrutinizing gaze on Miss Sophy's face. "I'll go out, an' be thankful to ye for the kindness. I think it's more 'n likely I'll get on my feet quicker there 'n here. I ain't so very bad hurt, 'n' 's soon 's I'm able to be round, I'll work out all I owe ye, ma'am, for the 'commodation."

Miss Sophy laughed in spite of herself.

"I ain't takin' you's a boarder," she said. "As soon as you are able to be round, I'll make a bargain with you, if you're a mind to, to look after the ranch. I think you 're about the sort of man I want out there, — that is, if we can agree about terms," added Miss Sophy, her shrewd business habit returning to her; "there will be time enough to talk about that when you 're up and out."

Zeph smiled faintly. "We ain't likely to disagree about terms, ma'am," he said. "I don't rate myself over 'n' above high. I 've got a good team, though, 'n' wagon, if they 'd be any use to ye."

"Have you?" exclaimed Miss Sophy. "The very thing I was needing. One of the farm horses has broken down, an' Waters said I 'd have to buy another. That is lucky," — and Miss Sophy chuckled to herself at this speedy returning of the bread she had cast on the waters, — "that is downright lucky. You can be carried out in your own team, and Waters 'll work one o' your horses right in harvestin' the wheat, 'n' that 'll save me buyin' a horse, 'n' be

a good deal more 'n your board to me, which 'll
set your mind to rest about that part on 't. I
always did hate to have anything to do with
horses; don't know anything about 'em, if I did
grow up on a farm; never could learn to har-
ness 'em; don't know a bad one from a good
one ; expect I'm cheated every time. I dare
say you'll find there's nothin' the matter with
this one Waters says 's sick. When you get
out there you can begin to keep your eye on
Waters 's soon 's you 're a mind to. You don't
need to be on your feet to do that, 'n' he needs
watchin'. "

A most injudicious confidence this to put in
a stranger, and a thing wholly foreign to Miss
Sophy's habitual way of talking with persons
whom she did not know. She could not account for it to herself, and felt a half embar-
rassment in her own presence, as it were, as
she realized it. With an unconscious effort at
reassuring her self-respect, she turned to the

doctor, as they left the house together, and said, "I don't know how it is, but there's something about that fellow makes you trust him 'on sight,' as you say on money notes. Don't you think he's all right?"

"No doubt of it," replied the doctor, heartily. "No doubt of his being's honest's the day is long; but I don't believe he's much force."

"How could he help having force, with that great body o' his?" said Miss Sophy, ingenuously, coloring as she spoke. "He's 'most a giant."

"I didn't mean that kind of force," laughed the doctor, privately amused at Miss Sophy's standard. "Some of the smallest men I've ever known have had the most force. I don't know much about this man. Nobody says any harm of him, though. But that wife of his is a regular devil! He's a fool to stick to her's he does."

Miss Sophy cast her eyes down. "But he's

married to her," she said. "What's he goin' to do?"

"Do!" shouted the doctor. And he thought to himself, "Well! of all queer questions for a steady-going old maid like Sophy Burr to ask! Do!" he repeated. "Why, get a divorce from her quicker 'n lightning! That's what he'd do if he'd got the force you was talking about."

"Perhaps he doesn't think that would be right," persisted Miss Sophy in a still lower voice, still with downcast eyes. They had been walking fast, and had just reached her gate, and as she said these last words she lifted the latch and held it in her fingers, nervously slipping it up and down. "Gammer Stein says he loves her spite of all she's done."

The doctor stared in undisguised amazement. "Loves her!" he ejaculated.

"Yes," said Miss Sophy; "so Gammer Stein

says, and that is the reason he was down there;
he follows her wherever she goes."

"Well, he is a fool, then," said the doctor.
"Beg your pardon, Miss Sophy. The word
slipped out unawares to me; but that's what
he is!"

"I suppose most folks would call him so,"
answered Miss Sophy, conveying her faint last
retaliation and championship in a slight emphasis on the word "most" as she closed the
gate.

"I should say so," retorted the doctor stiffly,
walking away with a puzzled sense of sudden
antagonism towards Miss Sophy, and a general
disposition to reflect contemptuously on spinster views of life. "I should say so!" he muttered to himself again. "What ever has got
into Sophy Burr, to be standing up for that
kind of immorality!"

And probably nothing short of a revelation
from Heaven could have made it apparent to

the good doctor's mind that it was not at all
for immorality that Miss Sophy was "standing up."

In the cool air and peaceful stillness of the
Greenhills ranch Zeph mended by the hour,
mended so fast that it seemed to him like a
miracle, mended spiritually as well as bodily;
new resolution, new purpose, awoke within him;
clouds lifted, and he saw clearly what he ought
to do. This new vision and purpose wrote
themselves at once in his face. It was little
less than a transformation. So great was the
change, that when one morning Miss Sophy
saw him driving up to her gate in the Greenhills wagon, she did not know him. It was not
quite two weeks since the day she had seen him
lying wan and spiritless in his bed.

"Sakes alive!" she ejaculated, "that can't be
Zeph Riker! 'T is too! Well, I never! He 's
more of a man than I thought." And there was
a certain indefinable tribute of new respect in her

manner as she greeted him with friendly kindness. "How you have picked up! I did n't know you at first. Ready to go to work, ain't you? You look as if you was!"

"Yes, ma'am," said Zeph. "I'm feelin' fustrate now; I'm ready to take hold o' anythin' ye 've got for me to do, 'n' very thankful to you, ma'am, for givin' me the chance. I expect ye 've got the right to me; the doctor he was a tellin' me to-day that he 'd about giv' me up when you come along that day 'n' took me out to your place."

"Pshaw!" said Miss Sophy. "That 's all nonsense. There was a dozen dead men in you then! You come in, and I 'll tell you what I want you to do. I 'm goin' to put a good deal of responsibility on you, 'n' I don't expect you 'll disappoint me."

"I 'll try not to," said Zeph, gravely. "I sha'n't cheat ye; but I might disap'int ye, for all that. There 's those that 'd answer for me

not cheatin' ye, if ye 'd like a reference, or somethin' o' the kind," he added.

" No ! " replied Miss Sophy. " I 'll take you
on your own references — and mine ! I ain't
often mistaken in folks, 'n' I made up my mind
the first night I saw you that I 'd like to get
you to work for me."

As soon as the words had passed her lips she
would have given much to recall them. The
effect they produced upon Zeph was pitiful to
see. In the flash of a second his face altered.
Bitter memories swept over him. His whole
figure seemed to droop, to lose strength ; he
looked again the grief-stricken, wandering, vacillating man who had fumbled weakly at her door
that night.

But it passed. In the few moments during
which Miss Sophy stood, embarrassed, dumb,
wondering at her own thoughtlessness in having
thus reminded him of his sorrow, Zeph had
wrestled himself free from the sudden grasp of

it, and looking her straight in the eyes, said: "I'm more to be trusted now than I was then, Miss Burr. I was pretty near out o' my mind that night. But I know where I stand now, an' I'm goin' to work. I'm all right, ma'am."

"That's all right, all right," exclaimed Miss Sophy, awkwardly. She did not intend to have any further implication with Zeph's domestic miseries. "If he's going to be my overseer 'n' run that ranch," said the shrewd woman to herself, "he's just got to be my overseer 'n' nothin' else. I can't be carryin' all his troubles on my shoulders. Now he's on his feet, he'll have to steer his own canoe."

It was only the helpless that appealed to Miss Sophy. People who were, as she in concise metaphor expressed it, "on their feet" must look out for themselves. She did, and she expected everybody else to. A very odd mixture of sympathy and hardness, compassion and coldness, was Miss Sophy. Even to herself

she was puzzling, — so swept away from her
bearings sometimes by great waves of pity
and desire to help her fellow-beings, and again
flintily indifferent to suffering, whose shape or
phase antagonized her common sense. There
was no limit to her benevolent activity, generosity, when once her heart was touched; but
she was quite capable of dismissing other cases
with a curt, "I 've no patience with such people,
— no patience at all! They deserve to suffer.
Good enough for them!"

But to keep Zeph her "overseer 'n' nothin'
else" proved not to be so easy as Miss Sophy
had thought; and the burden of the thought of
his sorrows would not roll off her shoulders as
she had intended. Do her best, she could not
shake herself free of a haunting consciousness
of his trouble and a growing admiration for his
courageous patience. No word of allusion to it
passed between them. She would not ask, and
nothing would have been further from Zeph's

impulse than to offer, any information in regard
to the state of affairs; but she fell into the habit
of studying his face, and drawing from its expression her own conclusions as to the posture
of matters. When he looked cheery and resolute, and spoke with vivacity, she said to herself,
" Well, he's gettin' along with it wonderfully."
Whenever he looked downcast and was silent,
saying only what was needful to be said, wrath
shook her inmost soul, and her soliloquies were
vindictive. " She's been pesterin' him, I know
she has, the hussy! I'd like to see her
drummed out o' town!" or "I expect he's
worryin' himself to death about those children.
I don't believe but the law'd give 'em to him if
he'd set about it. He could have the boy out
at the ranch 's well as not, an' the baby could
be boarded. I don't know what the Lord sends
children to such women for!"

Ah, very far was Miss Sophy drifting from
the purpose she had laid down to herself of

letting the overseer of her ranch " steer his own canoe"! She was fast nearing the pass of being ready to snatch from his hands both rudder and oars. It is a dangerous thing for a woman to thus study and pity a man. By paths of whose bearing she does not so much as dream, she is approaching a country whose name, if it were once pronounced in her ears, would terrify her. But there is no one to pronounce the name; the paths are winding; no guide-posts are there; no tokens; not so much as a dropped leaf to show who last went through. Shrewdest of all commanders in the world is Love, who makes his recruits recruit themselves.

If Miss Sophy had been told in these days that this constant, half-tender, half-impatient, half-pitying, half-wrathful watch and interest she was keeping up in Zeph's affairs was carrying her straight and fast into loving him, she would have been ready to slay her informant, and would have been sure the tale was a lie. All the same it was true. This was what was coming to Miss Sophy; helpless, unaware, stout-hearted, sturdy, independent, as she was, it was coming to her, and she did not know it; in her ignorance she was inviting it, making ready for it, feeding it. A mighty passion it would be when once it had Miss Sophy fairly in its clutch; no half-way measure or measures in anything Miss Sophy did, or became.

And so the days wore on, faster than ever, it seemed to her; with this new absorbing interest added to her other duties, she appeared to somehow lose time out of each day, and never, as she phrased it, "get round." From morning to night she went about her work with her brown straw hat pressed tight down on her forehead. This hat was always to Miss Sophy's servants a weather-signal. It had hitherto been her habit to wear it only on days of extra work, — house-cleaning, or the refitting of a room, moving of a stove, or some such exigency. The sight of it always struck terror to her workwomen's hearts. "When Miss Sophy comes down in the morning with her brown hat on," one of them once said, "we jest know we've got to look out an' step lively!" But this summer the brown hat was worn day after day, till gradually it lost its portentous meaning to the household. It really was no less a symptom of perturbations than before, but they were perturbations whose existence no one suspected, — least of all, Miss Sophy.

The summer had gone and the autumn had begun. October, with its hasty scurrying snows and threatening sleets, took Miss Sophy by surprise. "Goodness!" she cried one morning; "if it ain't snowing a'ready! Of all climates ever I heard of, I do think this Colorado's the most unreasonable. It's bad enough to keep on snowing into May; but to begin again the first week in October is a little too much! It don't seem but yesterday I had the stoves took down, an' now they 've all got to be set up again. It 's as bad as Vermont, every bit."

"Why don't you go to South California, Miss Sophy?" said one of her boarders, a young engineer, who had recently come from San Diego. "That 's the climate of all the world; never a flake of snow from one year's end to the other; flowers blooming out of doors all winter."

"Really? Truly?" said Miss Sophy, turning a wondering look at him. "I did n't know as 't was so warm 's that."

"It is n't," the engineer replied, laughing. "That 's the joke of it. I never suffered more with cold here than I have there, when I 've got caught out in the mountains at night; but it is n't cold by the thermometer, and that 's what the plants go by, I suppose; at any rate, I know they 're in bloom all winter, and I 've seen barley in full head in January."

"And never any snow, honest, now?" asked Miss Sophy, incredulously.

"Never," he replied; "that is, never except on the mountains. Once I saw a few flakes come down in Los Angeles; it was in February; it lasted about ten minutes, and everybody in town was out looking at it. There had n't been a flake seen there for nine years."

"That's where I'd like to live, then!" ejaculated Miss Sophy. "I guess I'll move."

"Many a true word's spoken in jest, Miss Sophy," laughed the young man as he left the table. "I dare say I'll see you there yet."

"You'll see me in the moon first!" retorted Miss Sophy. "It's my destiny to live an' die in Pendar Basin!" And she honestly thought so.

V.

GREENHILLS was shut up; the cows stabled in town and turned out daily to the meagre winter pasture with the town herd; the horses also, Zeph having represented to Miss Sophy that this would be far her best plan; it was nonsense keeping the ranch house open all winter, he said.

"Just cuttin' himself right out o' bread an' butter," thought Miss Sophy. "That's the kind o' man I knew he was. But what will you do, Zeph?" she said.

"Oh, I shall do very well," he replied. "I've got my house, and there is always teamin' to do, and odd jobs o' carpenterin'; they say there'll be considerable buildin' here this winter."

Building! Ah! the word reminded Miss Sophy. She had long wanted to build an

addition to her house; she had more than once
had estimates made for it, but had given it up
on account of the exorbitant price — or so it
seemed to her — asked by the builders. Here
was her chance.

"I want some buildin' done," she said. "I 've
been wantin' it for a long time. I suppose
you 'd as soon carpenter by the month as do
anything else?"

"I would sooner do anything for you, Miss
Burr, than do anything else," replied Zeph, with
an unconscious emphasis on the "you" which
made Miss Sophy feel ashamed of the under-
current of avariciousness in her proposition.

The plans were soon drawn, the materials pro-
cured, and Zeph's winter work was begun. And
now began also new and undreamed-of experiences in Miss Sophy's breast. Nothing was
more natural than that she should be in frequent consultation with her builder, should be
continually taking a look at the progress of the

building; this she would have done, whoever had been laboring on her new rooms. But to no other man's hammer would she have listened as she did to Zeph's. Not a sound of it escaped her ear; if she had been a poet she could have sung a strange song of the things it seemed to say: every vibration its steady stroke made in the air seemed to her to be telling the story of his sad life and his patient goodness. When it stopped, she wondered what he was doing, and often ran in to see. Hour by hour, day by day, she listened to and studied the building up of the walls, the laying of the floors.

"I 'most think I could build a house myself, I 've watched you so, Zeph," she said one day.

"I reckon there 's nothin' you could n't do, if you was to try, Miss Burr," replied Zeph, as he stepped back from a window-sill he was fitting and half shut his eyes to see if it were straight. "There ain't many women like you." And Zeph sighed. Women were to him a terrible problem. He was an innocent-minded man by nature, and had remained so spite of rough surroundings. His own experience of the falsity of a fair face and cooing voice had made him not so much bitter as afraid. He could not read the riddle. What was there in a woman to make her such an embodiment of heaven or of hell to a man? Zeph did not like to look any fair woman in the eye since he knew what Rushy was at heart. As for Miss Sophy, — poor Miss Sophy! — into his meditations on her the thought of sex seldom entered. He thought of her only as a force, — a helping, guiding, protecting personality. Perhaps his thoughts of her might have formulated themselves, even yet, somewhat as they did when he crouched in the church pew in instinctive fear of her "dreadful" activity. But by whatever name or trait she stood in his mind, she possessed the grateful loyalty of his steadfast nature. He had no phrases for this sentiment; neither avowed, measured, nor questioned it; he simply acted it. A doubt as to the fealty and service he owed to her no more occurred to him than a doubt as to the love he bore to his children. Money could not have bought from him one hour for which Miss Sophy had need or use. This was simply the man's instinct; the way he was made; he did not know that there was anything out of the ordinary in it. Persons of this order do not analyze either their own or other men's motives. They simply are what they are, and live their lives out day by day. They are spared much which more subjective natures suffer of perplexity and pain. But sometimes when a blow strikes them they are shivered to the ground as fatally as a tree is rent by a lightning · shaft or uprooted by a sudden blast. And when this happens, nobody knows what did it. People wonder of what they have died.

A dim knowledge of some such quality as this in Zeph was slowly filtering into Miss Sophy's perception.

"He has n't ever got over it," she said to herself as she went stirring about the house, quite unaware that she was always thinking of Zeph. "He has n't ever got over it, 'n' I don't suppose he ever will. If he 'd only get the children with him he 'd stand it better. I should n't wonder if 't was the death o' the man yet! The hussy!"

Perhaps if Miss Sophy had not been so absorbed in these reviewings of Zeph's situation and emotions she might have come sooner to the realization of her own. But she had no time to think of herself. She was forever groping, groping, like one in the dark; half blinded by pity and by a stinging sense of the utter impotence of all outside help for this sorrowing man whose life had been so strangely set side by side with her own.

However, the groping days were nearly over. They could not last forever. Such situations clear themselves by laws no less fixed than the laws which determine the joining and the separating of chemical elements. Events combined to help on the clearing up. Strange things had been happening to Zeph of which Miss Sophy knew nothing, and never would have known except for her half ally and confidante in regard to him, Gammer Stein.

Miss Sophy and Gammer had seen each other seldom of late. The winter had been a severe one, with frequent snows and bitter cold; a foot of snow was to Gammer a more absolute barrier than a stone wall; and to Miss Sophy the mercury at zero meant simply a stiffening of every faculty as well as every muscle. Her energy was in direct ratio to the warmth of the air; at ninety Fahrenheit she was in full vigor; even at a hundred she worked on with delight. In cold weather she grew inert and torpid, and used to say she would like to curl up like a spider and lie in a dark corner till spring.

Thus it had happened that nearly three months had gone by without her seeing Gammer; and one morning in March she said to herself, as she was washing the breakfast dishes, "I really must go and see Gammer to-day. If this wind 'll only stop blowin', I 'll go right after dinner." The words had hardly formed themselves in her thought, when, seeing a shadow darken the window, she looked up and saw Gammer herself at the door.

"I never!" said Miss Sophy aloud. "If that ain't speakin' o' angels, sure enough! There 's somethin' cur'us about its so often happenin' that way!"

"I was just this very minute sayin' to myself I 'd come up 'n' see you this afternoon, Gammer!" she exclaimed, as she opened the door. "I 'm real glad to see you."

"Then yer 've heered it!" gasped Gammer, sinking breathless into a chair.

"Heard what?" cried Miss Sophy, instantly alert, already, in her heart, sure it was something about Zeph. "I hain't heard anything. What 's happened?"

"Rushy Riker 's got her bill," cried Gammer. "She 's got it; 'n' she 'n' thet Nat wuz married last night."

"Married!" cried Miss Sophy. "What do you mean? How could she be married?"

"Why, she 's billed," retorted Gammer. "Ther papers come yisterday 't noon, 'n' she 'n' Nat wuz married last night. I allow ther won't nobody hev nothin' ter do with 'em, — nobody thet 's decent. I allow 't 's the dearest day's work ever she 's done 'n her life. Thet Nat 'll go off 'n' leave her some day; he 's none too good; 'n' she can't lay down on Zeph agen."

Miss Sophy stood like a statue, her face scarlet, her eyes flashing.

"Divorced!" she shrieked. "How 'd she ever get a divorce? There ain't a thing against that man, not one!"

"Ter be sure ther ain't," said Gammer, settling back in her chair. "I allow thar ain't no two sides ter thet; she couldn't hev got no bill ef he'd hev appeared agen it; but he would n't. He talked it over with me. She come up thar ter ther house 's long ago 's — wall, somewhar abaout New Year's, I allaow 't wuz, 'n' she told Zeph she wuz gwine to bill him 'n' marry Nat; 'n' he told her she could n't; 'n' she sez, sez she, ' I kin 'n' I will; 'n' 't any rate I 'm gwine ter live with Nat.' 'He 'll never marry ye, Rushy,' sez Zeph. ' He will too,' sez she; an' then, ef yer 'll b'leeve me, thet thar Zeph, — I swar, I donno ef the man 's flesh 'n' blood, er what he ez, — sez he, ' Ef he 'll marry yer, Rushy, I won't hender yer gettin' ther bill. Then yer kin live decent. But he 's got ter swar ter marry ye; ' 'n' I allaow ter yeow, the next night, ef they did n't both on 'em,

she 'n' Nat, the pizen skunk, — ef thar war n't
both on 'em thar to Zeph's, tellin' him what
they'd made up thar minds ter dew; 'n' naow
they've got 't done. Thet's the kind er law thar
ez in this hyar country; she's billed aout clar 'n'
free ez ef she'd been 'z decent ez enny woman
could be, 'n' he wuz ther one 't wuz wrong. He
jest never 'peared 't all. Thet wuz all they
wanted. I'd jest like ter see 'em both jugged!
I allaow ther would n't nothin' short er thet tech
'em. 'T wan't but er few nights sence, thar wuz
er dance, a real respectable dance, down thar
whar she lives, 'n' she 'n' Nat went in, 'n' thar
come up one o' ther managers, 'n' sez he, 'Yer'll
be ser good 's ter git aout er this room, 'n' be
mighty quick abaout et, tew, or yer'll git holped
aout;' 'n' they jest larfed, 'n' went aout a tossin'
thar heads ez high 'n' mighty. I allaow naow
they're married they'll brazen 't aout. Folks
forgits everythin'."

"Has she got the right to keep the children?"

asked Miss Sophy in a hoarse whisper. Her face was very pale now, and the flashing of her eye strangely dimmed.

"I did n't heer 't said," replied Gammer, "but she's got 'em. I allaow ef he did n't 'pear, the childen 'd go to her, same ez she got ther bill. 'N' he sez he 'd ruther she hed 'em; they 'll dew more fur her, he sez, 'n everythin' else. She 's allers good ter 'em. He 'll keep an eye ter 'em."

"Then he 's 's free to-day 's if he 'd never been married 't all," said Miss Sophy, still in a whisper, still pale, and with dimmed eyes.

"I allaow he ez," said Gammer; " 'n' I allaow ter yeow thet, much 's I 'm agen bills, 'n' billed folks marryin' agen, I 'd like ter see Zeph Riker git him another wife, pesky quick tew, jest ter spite them tew devils thet 's kep' him in er hell, 's yer might say, these tew years, goin' on three. Mebbe 't ain't right, 'n' mebbe 't is. I allaow I 'd take the resk on 't ef 't wuz me."

And now a startling thing occurred. Miss

Sophy, who had been standing, immovable, rigid, in front of Gammer, listening to this narrative, turning first red, then pale, and fast losing her self-control, suddenly lost it altogether, and flinging herself into a chair, buried her face in her hands, and burst into tears, sobbing out, half apologetically, " I never heard such a story in my life ! Such things never happened where I was brought up."

Gammer was astounded. Miss Sophy's bearing, her attitude throughout all her active interest in Zeph's affairs, had always been unmistakably that of the cool, common-sense, kindly benefactor. Her sudden change to the level of a weeping friend baffled Gammer's utmost powers of understanding. Bewilderment made her dumb. Finally she stammered : " I allaow yer tired, mebbe. I git plum beat aout sometimes, 'n' ther leastest thing 'll set me off cryin'." At which Miss Sophy cried harder than ever, and Gammer's bewilderment deepened.

At last Miss Sophy, recovering herself, said:
"That's so. This long spell o' cold weather 's
got my nerves all strung up, somehow, so I
can't bear anything; an' I'm sure it's enough
to make anybody cry, to think what that man's
gone through with. I've got to know him real
well, you see, havin' him here this winter to
work on the addition," she added.

"Yes," said Gammer, glad to change to a less
exciting topic. "He wuz er tellin' us abaout it.
He allowed he hed reel pleasure buildin' it fur
ye. He sets a heap by yer; donno 's yer know
it, but he doos. He sez thar war n't never sech
er woman 'n the world ez yeow be."

Miss Sophy's cheeks were red again, and
her eyes, brighter than before, fastened on Gammer's face as she spoke these words, — fastened
there with an expression which the honest old
woman was far from understanding.

Miss Sophy had had a revelation. No more
disguise, equivocation, illusion, ignorance, on

her part, in regard to her feeling toward Zeph. She loved him, and she knew it.

What would come of it? Nothing; she said to herself sternly, — nothing could come of it. The man's heart was not his own, was no longer to be won by any woman; it had been given once for all, and he was not a man to love twice, said Miss Sophy in her simplicity, — given once for all to that wretched, wicked woman, the mother of his children, who had now separated herself from him forever. It was bitter. But there were consolations. Very well Miss Sophy knew that his life would not be severed from hers unless she herself chose; that they would work together, her interests the same to him as his own, her wishes and needs determining his daily duties, and, what was still more, the sight of her, and talking with her, the greatest comfort and happiness left to his saddened life. This was a great deal. With this, Miss Sophy thought she could be contented.

"And if I can't, I can go away," she said to herself. All this and much more had passed through her mind while she was saying her final words of parting with Gammer, who had, as she phrased it, "dropped everything 'n' run to tell the noos on 't," and was in haste to get home.

After Gammer had gone, Miss Sophy turned her back on her work, and locked herself into her room for a resolute thinking. She did not mince matters with herself any more than she would have done with another.

" Here you are, Sophy Burr," she said, as she would have said it aloud to a culprit standing bodily before her. " Here you are ! Now what? " At the end of the hour she was no nearer knowing. Her second soliloquy had closed, like her first, with the words, " If I can't, I can go away."

The March snows, and the April snows, and the May snows, came and went. June followed

like a midsummer close on their icy days, and
Greenhills was green again. Young vegetables
were peering up in the garden; the cows were
revelling in fresh grass; and Zeph, back at his
post on the ranch, was proud of the cream and
butter he had for Miss Sophy twice a week.
On the face of things were prosperity and
peace in both Miss Sophy's houses. Zeph's
countenance wore a new look of contentment
and calm. He had put behind him the things
that were dead, and was pressing forward to the
things that remained alive, in way of duty and
work.

A change had come about in his relations
with Miss Sophy, which had given him a new
self-respect, and a sense of manly indepen-
dence, which were an ever-present stimulus
and pleasure. He did not clearly know how
this had happened. Miss Sophy knew. It
had begun by her calling him "Mr. Riker"
one day.

Startled and uneasy, he looked at her,—looked the question he did not speak. Miss Sophy laughed. Relieved, he exclaimed, " Ye scared me, Miss Burr. I was afraid I'd 'fended ye."

" Oh, no ! " said the clever Miss Sophy. " Far from it. But I don't feel it's respectful for me to go on calling a man by his first name, when he manages all my affairs for me. I look to you for 'most everything now, and I ain't goin' to call you Zeph any longer."

" 'Most everybody does," said Zeph.

" That's because they don't know you so well as I do," said Miss Sophy.

All the way out to Greenhills Zeph kept thinking this over. It puzzled him. He was pleased, and yet not pleased. It seemed to put him farther from Miss Sophy, and yet nearer. He gave up trying to understand the mystery of it. On the whole, however, he wished that she would say " Zeph." But she did not, — not for many a day.

The next thing Miss Sophy did was simply an act of justice. She said to him one day, " Mr. Riker, at the rate you are going on, you will double the value of my ranch for me. I can see that. You are working as if you were working for yourself."

" Of course," said Zeph, simply.

" Well," continued Miss Sophy, " that 's a thing money does n't pay for. Wages don't cut any figure at all when a man takes hold of a place that way; you ought to have a share in the place. Now, what I 've been thinking would be a fairer way, would be for me to reckon your year's wages in a lump as so much put into the ranch on your account, so we shall be owning it together; do you understand? And if you want to go into stock a little more, why I 'll go shares in that too."

Zeph stared. The good luck of the thing amazed him. Yet he saw that there was a certain fairness in it. Miss Sophy was not making

him a gift, only helping him to a good investment of his earnings.

He did not make any profuse expressions of
gratitude. It was not his way. But his "Thank
you, Miss Burr, I could n't ask for anythin'
better 'n that if I 'd had my choice given t' me,"
was all that Miss Sophy needed. And the new
life and spirit in him which dated from that day
were also new life and spirit to her affectionate
soul.

Good as it was for Zeph to be called Mr.
Riker, he did not like it. At last it seemed to
him he could not bear it. Vainly he wondered
at the intensity of his feeling in regard to it.
"What odds does 't make what she calls me?
I swear it 's queer how I hate to hear her say
Mr. Riker t' me," he said.

Finally he mustered courage to say this. It
was at Miss Sophy's back gate; he had come in
as usual with the Greenhills butter and cream,
and a fine lot of green peas, the first of the

season, — and Greenhills peas were always two weeks ahead of anybody's else in the region. Miss Sophy was delighted, and as she bade him good-by, she said, " I 'm proud enough, to have peas so early. I can't see how you did it. I 'm ever so much obliged to you, Mr. Riker."

" My name 's Zeph," said Zeph, in a sudden impulse of desperate courage.

" So 's mine Sophy," retorted Miss Sophy, in an equally sudden impulse of desperate courage, looking full into his eyes.

" Why! Miss Burr!" gasped Zeph, dropping the reins in his agitation. But Miss Sophy had turned and run up the path as fast as her feet could carry her, laughing, however, and looking back at Zeph, who sat gazing after her in consternation.

" Good Lord!" he said to himself as she disappeared in the doorway. " What did she mean? She wan't mad, anyhow. She could n't ha' meant I was to call her Sophy! O' course it could n't ha' been that!"

"What did she mean?" was a constant refrain in Zeph's thoughts for the next three days; and, "I wonder what he 'll do when he comes in Thursday?" was the refrain in Miss Sophy's. And when Thursday morning came, and the Greenhills wagon was seen turning into the lane at the back of Miss Sophy's house, her heart thumped like a hammer in her bosom.

"If he don't call me Sophy now, he never will," she thought.

Zeph was also in trepidation. "I dassent open my mouth," he thought, "till she 's said something first. Perhaps she 's forgotten all about it."

She met him on the porch. The instant he looked in her face, he knew she had not forgotten. The instant Miss Sophy looked in his, she divined his thought; divined also that it would be hers, and not his, to speak the first word.

"Good morning," she said; and after a second's pause, "Is it to be Mr. Riker, then, or Zeph?"

"Zeph," he said, in a voice so low it seemed less than a whisper. "I can't bear it, somehow, to have ye call me anythin' else."

"Well, then, Zeph it is," replied Miss Sophy, as lightly and glibly as if she had nothing more at stake than a jest of an idle moment; "but you know what I told you. If Zeph's your name, Sophy's mine. Give and take's fair play."

Zeph's hands were full — his hands and arms also — of parcels from Greenhills: the butter, the jug of cream, young radishes, lettuce, peas. He did not speak, but went on slowly laying them down one by one, trying to think what he should say.

"Well?" said Miss Sophy. "Bargain?"

Her light tone deceived him. "I can't think ye'd make fun o' me, Miss Burr," he said. "I don't make out your meanin'."

"I couldn't ever make fun of you, Mr. Riker," retorted Miss Sophy, in a tone still merry, but with an under note in it which Zeph had not been man if he had failed to perceive.

"You're the best friend I ever had, or ever shall have, in this world," cried Zeph.

"And you're the best friend I have, or ever expect to have, in this world," answered Miss Sophy; "the very best — Zeph!"

Their eyes met, — Miss Sophy's shining with resolution and tears, Zeph's, dark with unfathomable emotion and bewilderment. He opened his lips to speak; then slowly shaking his head, turned to go.

"Good-by, Zeph!" said Miss Sophy, smiling. She had conquered, she was sure. It would not be on that day, or the next, perhaps, that Zeph could speak her name, but it would come.

"If you can't say Sophy, you need n't say

anything," she continued. "I don't like Miss Burr any better than you do Mr. Riker!"

Zeph's eyes lighted up. His tongue was loosed now. "Don't ye?" he exclaimed. "If I thought that, I could learn any name ye wanted me to!"

"Sophy 'll do," said Miss Sophy, dryly. "It's as good as Zeph. They ain't either of 'em any great beauties 'o names to boast of!" And now they both laughed merrily, and parted without another word, only a farewell smile to each other, — a smile out of which all the sparkle of the mirthful laughter had gone, leaving behind the soft light of a deep affection. And the next time the Greenhills wagon came in (it was but three days from Thursday to Monday), Miss Sophy met it at the gate, and said with sweet gravity, "Good-morning, Zeph;" and Zeph made answer, "Good-morning, Sophy." And it would have been hard to say which of them was the happier in the new sound the syllables bore and the new bond their speaking made.

The happiness of it lasted Miss Sophy for many days; but as the summer wore away she began to look for something more, — she hardly dared phrase to herself for what, yet in her heart she knew ; and knew, too, that the thing she craved was hers by right; that the lonely, sorrowful, deserted man for whom she had come to care so tenderly had come also to love her with a true devotion. But gradually there grew up in her a fear that he would never say so. Not by word or look did he show that any idea of any relation beyond or different from their present one was in his mind. Whether it were that he lacked courage, or that he still held himself bound by the bond which his wife had broken, Miss Sophy could not determine. On the latter point she herself had had doubts, but by some surreptitious reading on the subject of divorce, and by several cautiously conducted consultations with her minister and with other persons, she had at length become fully satisfied that there could be no possible shadow of wrong in the second marriage of a man whose wife had not only betrayed and deserted him, but become legally the wife of another.

"It has n't got any business to stand in his way one minute," she said to herself again and again; "and perhaps 't ain't that that is standing in his way. But what else can it be? 'T ain't any love for her; I'm sure o' that. That's one comfort!"

And by the help of this last item of comfort Miss Sophy weathered the summer fairly well. But when the autumn signals were flung out, — great yellow patches of aspens high up on the mountain-sides, and tossing plumes of purple asters around the Greenhills spring, — Miss Sophy lost heart.

"Winter 'll be here in a jiffy," she said, "an' he won't let me keep the ranch open, an' I can't stand it; I can't stand not to see him 's I 've been seein' him!" And Miss Sophy racked her brain vainly for a device.

Finally one occurred to her, — so desperate, so final, it almost took her breath away as it first flashed through her thoughts; but the longer she thought, the more she believed it good. It was desperate, and it would be final: if she won, she won; if she lost, she lost — all. This is a common trick of Love's winning. He makes gamesters, desperate gamesters, of most of us at least once in our lives. We throw down our last card and bravely call out color or number, all the while feeling a death-grip at our throats.

"I might as well!" said Miss Sophy. "There's no use going on this way forever. It's nonsense; besides that, it'll kill me. I can't stand it. I'd rather go away."

And she made up her mind. But after she had made it up, she hesitated day after day. She trembled. More than once she opened her

lips to speak the words, and terror held her
dumb. If she lost, she lost all.

At last she spoke. It was at Greenhills.
Already the foreshadowing of winter glooms
had touched the place; frost had turned the
vines black and shrivelled every leaf in the
garden. Yet it was only the middle of Sep-
tember. It looked desolate.

"Looks as I feel," said Miss Sophy, grim and
resolute; "but I'll feel worse, mebbe, before
I'm done with it."

"Zeph," she said. Zeph was standing by
her side at the bars of the corral where all
the yearlings had been put. He had been
pointing them out to her with great satisfaction.

There was something in Miss Sophy's tone
which fell strangely on Zeph's ear. He knew
the inflections of her voice better than she
dreamed. What was coming? She had never
pronounced his name thus before. Never, in-

deed! He turned his face quickly towards her, inquiringly.

"Zeph!" she said again, and again the words refused to come. She took firm hold of the upper rail of the fence to support herself, and began once more: "Zeph, I've made up my mind to go to California. I'm goin' to sell out an' go this fall. I about made up my mind last winter I'd never stand another o' these Colorado winters; but it's been so pleasant this summer, it kind of put me out o' the notion; but now I see it settin' in again I feel just 's I did, 'n' I'm goin'! I'm gettin' too old to stand any more snow. Do you know anybody that ud like to buy this ranch? There's a man ready to take
· the other house right off my hands just as 't is, furniture 'n' all."

Astonishment, incredulity, pain, bewilderment, each in turn and all together, had swept over Zeph's face while Miss Sophy was speaking these words. His eyes fastened themselves on hers blankly. As soon as she ceased speaking, he stammered: "Sophy! you! going to California! goin' away! You can't mean it, Sophy! What are ye goin' for? You're doin' splendid here!" The words came slower and slower; the man was half stunned; and before the hesitating sentences were concluded, he, too, had instinctively grasped the bars for support. "Ye can't mean it, Sophy! I 'most think ye're crazy."

"I guess not," said Miss Sophy, more at ease already. If he felt it like this, he would never let her go alone, surely. Her winning must be close at hand. She did not yet thoroughly know the nature of the man she was dealing with.

"I guess not," she repeated. "I hain't ever had the name o' bein' light-headed. I've been a long time makin' up my mind to this."

"I wish ye'd ha' let me know on 't sooner," said Zeph, in an aggrieved tone, which was music to Miss Sophy's ears.

"Why?" she said.

"I could ha' got used t' 't by degrees," he replied sadly. "It's struck me all of a heap. But I'll do all I can to help ye, Sophy," he continued, bracing himself up, and looking away from her for a minute. "I could ha' got a buyer for the ranch better in the summer than now. It's a bad time to sell. I expect it would be better to let it lay 's 't is till spring. I can look after it for ye till then, same 's I have done." And Zeph sighed.

Alas! Had she lost? What was Miss Sophy to say next? The talk had taken a hopeless turn. To gain time, she replied meaninglessly: "I don't know! I suppose 't is a bad time! I never thought o' that. But I want to go before the cold weather sets in. There's flowers all winter long in the south part o' California, they say; an' that's where I'm goin'."

"Ye 've always seemed real happy here, Sophy," cried Zeph, "'n' real well too! 'T never

so much 's crossed my mind ye 'd ever leave;
ye ain't got nothin' ailin' ye, have ye, to make
ye need to go?" And his face clouded over
with the new anxiety which had that instant
occurred to him.

What tantalizing cruelty sometimes in these
impenetrable veils between human hearts, which
are at other times such merciful protection! If
Miss Sophy could have known that as Zeph
asked this question his racked heart was saying, " If she 's got any disease hold on her I 'll
coax her t' let me go 'long too, 'n' take care of
her," she would have then and there feigned
herself the victim of any known malady. But
in her pride of energetic health she made haste
to repudiate any such implication.

"Mercy, no!" she said. "Do I look like
a sick woman? Never felt better. But I 'm
tired o' this place, an' this life, an' everything
about it, an' especially o' these winters. I 'd
like to go where I 'd never see another flake o'

snow 's long 's I live. I was brought up on
snow; 'n' I 've had six months o' snow — that is
o' bein' liable to snow — out o' every year I 've
been here; 'n' I 'm sick on 't, 'n' I 'm goin'.
I 've got enough to get me a place that I can
make a livin' off anywhere; 'n' I don't know
any reason why I should slave myself here, 'n'
freeze to death every winter."

Luckless Miss Sophy. Each one of these last
sentences went like a bullet to Zeph's heart.
" Tired o' this place," was she? The place
which had seemed to him almost blissful of
late; and the work which they had been jointly
doing, he and she, the fruitful ranch, the increasing herd, the prosperous boarding-house,
—all this was to her " slaving to death," and
she was going. She had made up her mind to
it without a word to him any more than if he had
been the poorest cattle-herder, on the ranch, —
to him, to whom she had said, only a few short
months ago, that he was the best friend she had

on the earth! Very well! woman like woman!
They were all the same, heartless and untrue, —
one from vanity and passion, another from ca-
price! They were all alike! This was the last
woman whom he would ever trust! The storm
of all these bitter thoughts turned Zeph's face
stern and his voice cold, and when he replied
curtly, "Well, ye 'd better go, then, if that 's the
way ye feel, Sophy," poor Miss Sophy had to
clutch tight to her rail to keep from staggering.

The hurt that he gave her, however, was their
salvation. Without it they might have perhaps
parted forever, then and there, neither knowing
that the other was wounded. But this hurt was
too sudden and too deep to be borne without
a cry; and Miss Sophy's voice, even without
the tears in her eyes, would have appealed to
any man like a cry, as she exclaimed, "Oh,
Zeph! I don't see why you take it that way!
I think you 're real cruel!"

"I don't never mean to be that," said Zeph,

" not to nobody. But you don't seem to think it's anythin' for a fellow to be turned off all in a minute, an' everythin' all broke up!"

Miss Sophy took heart again. "Who said anything about turning off?" she asked, with a faint smiling in her tearful eyes.

"Well, you didn't say anythin' about anythin' else!" retorted Zeph, still sullen. "You hadn't any idee o' takin' me with ye?"

"I've been thinkin' all the time, Zeph," said Miss Sophy, "that I didn't know how I'd ever get along without you!"

"Why didn't ye say so, then?"

"How could I?"

"How could ye? What's to hender? Ye got me to do your business for ye here, 'n' let on to think so much o' my managin'; 'n' why couldn't ye 've said ye 'd like to have me keep on with it there? No, ye 're tired o' the place 'n' everybody in it! That 's what 's the matter with you!"

Was this Zeph? What was to become of
Miss Sophy in this chaos of confusion which
she had drawn down on her head? Stretching
out both her hands, she cried: "Zeph, I don't
know what's got into you 'n' me to be quarrellin' here, nor what we're quarrellin' about,
neither. I should think you'd know that the
last thing I'd want to do, would be to part from
you, an' that I'd rather have you manage for
me than anybody!"

The pleading in her voice was unmistakable;
her face glowed with affection. Still Zeph
seemed both deaf and blind.

"Then why didn't ye ask me to go 'long
too?" he reiterated. "Why didn't ye take
me into any o' your plans? Will you take
me now?" he added, with a half-surly and incredulous emphasis.

Miss Sophy hid her face in both her hands;
she was rosy red; she saw a vista opening.

"How could I, Zeph?" she whispered. "Folks

don't know us out there. It's very different
here, where everybody knows us. I don't want
to go without you, Zeph, you need n't think! "

Into the chambers of Zeph's brain light had
broken at last. What a dolt he had been!

" Oh, Sophy, Sophy! " he cried, " was ye a
tryin' me? I do believe ye was! " and he threw
his arms around her. " Sophy, it 'most killed
me to hear ye talk so cool o' goin' away 'n'
leavin' me, when I hain't had a thought, day
nor night, except o' servin' you 'n' belongin' to
you, for so long! "

"Well, why did n't you say so, then?" retorted
Miss Sophy, half laughing, half crying, making
haste to turn the tables on him and avenge herself. " Why did n't you say so, and not drive
me into just about offerin' myself to you? "

"Sophy! Sophy!" answered Zeph, "don't you
go to talkin' any such way 's that. I don't know
about offerin', 's you call it; givin' 's more 'n
offerin', an' you know well enough I giv' myself

to you a long ways back, an' hain't ever had, from that day to this, any idee o' doin' anythin' but helpin' ye an' lovin' ye 's long 's I live on this earth!"

And Miss Sophy was content.

VI.

THERE was but one drawback to Miss Sophy's happiness. In the new confidence which now existed between her and Zeph, she learned more fully than she had done before the depth of his affection for his children. She found that during all these months it had been his habit to see them frequently, — sometimes by clandestine watchings, sometimes by Rushy's consent that Zephie should on a Sunday take his little sister to their father's house. By this means Zeph had kept himself constantly in relation with them and retained strong influence over the boy. Separation from them was going to be a terrible thing to him; there were times when he even doubted if it were right for him to go away and leave them entirely in the control and at the mercy of their stepfather. Only his unshaken confidence in the strength of Rushy's maternal affection enabled him to think of it.

"She's just like a wildcat 'bout the chillen," he said, "an' always was; if Nat Leeson should so much's raise his hand to 'em, she'd leave him quicker 'n lightnin'. I ain't a mite afraid of his ever doin' 'em any harm that way. But if she should come to want any way, — Sophy, I don't see it clear just how to fix that. Ye know, Sophy, I'd always feel myself bound to those children."

"Of course!" replied Miss Sophy. "And so do I. I wish to goodness we had 'em both here this minute to take 'em with us! That's what I'd like!"

"Would ye, Sophy?" cried Zeph. "Would ye really? Oh, Sophy, ye 're real good!"

"I don't suppose there 'd be any chance o' gettin' 'em, or either one on 'em," said Miss Sophy. "Would there?"

"Oh, Lord!" cried Zeph, catching his breath at the very idea. "That's all ye know about Rushy! She'd rather kill 'em than let anybody else have 'em! She's fierce, Rushy is. There is n't the least use thinkin' o' such a thing."

But the doctrine that there was no use in thinking of a thing was not in Miss Sophy's creed. The more obstacles lay in the way, the more her native obstinacy allied itself with her indomitable courage to surmount them. And in this instance a passion greater than either the courage or the obstinacy came in, making a triple alliance strong enough to move mountains. Her love for Zeph was so great that its instincts were preternaturally keen.

"He'll never be happy long away from them children o' his," she said, "an' he's got to have 'em, — or at least the baby; she'd be more to him than the boy; he'd get along if he had her; an' if we got her, the boy'd be big enough to come before long if he wanted to."

Plan after plan, all visionary and impracticable, Miss Sophy revolved in her head. Actual kidnapping of the child would not have seemed to her wrong; but her common sense told her that it would involve dangers not to be thought of. Cautiously she sounded Gammer Stein as to the possibility of Rushy's being induced, by the prospects of superior advantages to her daughter, to give her to be adopted by a stranger. No suspicion crossed Gammer's mind as to Miss Sophy's personal interest in the matter, any further than her benevolent interest in Zeph explained it.

"Some o' yer folks wantin' to 'dopt a child?" she said. "Wall, I allow ef they know what's fur thar good they'll keep shy o' proposin' it to Rushy Riker, — Leeson, I s'pose her name is naow, but I sha'n't never call her nothin' but Riker, not outen Zeph wuz ter git married, an' I allow thet's ther furthest off from his thoughts 't ever wuz. He seems ter be reel

settled naow. 'T wuz luck fur him a gittin'
yeour place."

"Then you think that Mrs. Leeson would not
give up the little girl?" interrupted Miss Sophy,
who found the conversation both disagreeable
and embarrassing.

"Not she!" said Gammer. "I'll say thet
much fur Rushy Riker. Money couldn't buy
one o' her young uns, I allaow 't couldn't.
She's fierce fur 'em allers, an' reel good ter
'em, tew. She's a hussy, aout an' aout, an'
allers wuz, I be bound; but she's a good
mother t' her young uns ser fur's lovin' 'em
goes. She'd run round 'n' leave 'em fur frolics
an' sech, an' she ain't no great hand ter tidy 'em
up; but she loves 'em more 'n most women doos
thar young uns, I allaow she doos. Thet's one
thing made me ser sure Nat'd never marry her
'n ther livin' world, kase I allowed he wouldn't
be bothered 'th ther young uns; but 't wuz
young uns 'n' all, 'r else not 't all, 'n' it doos

look ez ef he wuz bound ter hev Rushy. He's workin' her 'most ter death tew; thet's what some says; 't wuz jest fur her cookin' he wanted her. He's took the restaurant now, — the Star restaurant, whar he wuz a cookin', 'n' he 'n' her ez runnin' it, 'n' er takin' in money like greased lightnin', they say. She's an orful good cook, Rushy ez. She's smart; nothin' she can't do ef she wants ter, 'cept be decent; I allow she could do thet tew, ef she wanted ter. She don't want ter. But she don't do no gaddin' naow, don't yer furgit it! She's got er marster naow 'stead o' er slave; thet's what she hed afore, — er reg'lar slave, thet Zeph wuz. She'll be sick o' her bargain, I allaow, 'fore she's through with it. I know a reel likely young un I allaow them folks could git, — it's a boy, though. 'T wuz a gal yer said they wuz wantin'?"

"Yes," said Miss Sophy, feeling guilty, but playing her game boldly. "It is a girl these parties want. I dare say they'll find one, though; children are plenty enough."

"More 'n enough, whar they ain't wanted," replied Gammer. "I allaow thet 's anuther queer thing ther Lawd doos. Hyar 's these yer folks o' yourn huntin' fur a child ter 'dopt, 'n' hyar daown 'n this yer very flairt I could p'int yer ter 's many 's twenty houses whar they'd be glad 'n' thankful ef thar wuz fewer chillen ter feed 'n' clothe. Thet 's ther way 't is. I allaow 't 's cur'us. But I could n't never see haow 't is folks wants ter 'dopt chillen. I allaow I could n't dew no sech thing 's thet."

"Why not?" asked Miss Sophy, so sharply that Gammer looked up in surprise.

"Wall, I allaow I could n't jest say why not," she replied. "It 's er kind er feelin' I hev; 'pears like 't would be a kinder cheatin' natur', somehow, thet would n't work."

"I don't think so at all," answered Miss Sophy. "It seems to me the most natural thing in the world for folks that have n't got any child o' their own, to adopt one."

"I expect it's hevin' chillen o' yer own makes 'doptin' 'em seem so cur'us," replied Gammer, placidly; "arter ye 've hed 'em, I allaow yer don't think much o' 'doptations. 'S fur 's I 'm concerned, I would n't durst trust myself with other folks's chillen. Chillen ez tryin'."

"I should think they must be," said Miss Sophy, turning to go, glad to escape from the conversation which booted nothing and made her uncomfortable.

Slowly, reluctantly, she abandoned her project as impracticable. It grieved her sorely, and it disquieted her anticipations of the future. But she saw no means, which she dared use, of bringing about the desired end. She did not stop thinking about it, however; that was out of her power. Many a night she lay awake far into the morning hours vainly pondering, wishing, regretting.

Her arrangements for leaving were nearly complete; so quietly and judiciously had she made them, that few persons in the town knew of her contemplated change; and to no one except her minister had she confided her intention of marrying Zeph.

"There's been talk enough about his affairs," she said, "an' it's nobody's business but his and mine what we're going to do." The marriage was to take place at the minister's house, with only the necessary witnesses, on the evening of their departure from town, and would not be known until she and Zeph were many miles away. They were going to take the long overland journey in their own wagon, in company with a party of emigrants who were about setting off from a mining town a few hours by rail south of Pendar Basin. This was Zeph's plan. He had long desired such a journey. When he proposed it to Miss Sophy, her first reply was, "Mercy, Zeph, it'd take forever!"

"Only about two months, Sophy," he said
pleadingly. "Two months out o' doors every
minute."

"Two months!" echoed Miss Sophy. "Is that
all? Well, I suppose that 'd be two honeymoons
'stead o' one!" And in this view the prospect
of the journey grew more and more pleasing to
her.

It only lacked a week of the day fixed for
starting. Greenhills was sold, and well sold,
and the money in the bank, — quite enough to
buy the new ranch in California, or wherever they
might determine to live. The people who had
bought Miss Sophy's boarding-house, furniture,
good-will, and so forth, had arrived and taken
possession, the transfer being made with sur-
prisingly little jar to the household. "It 's easy
enough to do anything if you once set about it,"
said Miss Sophy, never suspecting how uncom-
mon was the executive force within her which
made all the difference in the world in the way

of "setting about" things. It seemed odd to her
to be a boarder in her own home; and the hours
hung so heavily on her hands that she more than
once wished that she was at liberty to go into
the kitchen and cook the dinner. Zeph was away.
He had gone to make the arrangements for their
wagon journey, to have everything in readiness,
so that their wagons might be in waiting for
them at the railway station where they would
leave the cars. When this plan was made, it had
not occurred to Miss Sophy that it would distress her to be separated from Zeph for a few
days; but she was finding it intolerable. Except
for sheer shame, she would have followed him.
Her mind continually reverted to the grief of
her youth, the death of her first lover. "Folks
that belongs to each other hain't got any business takin' such risks," she soliloquized. "If
there was anythin' to happen to Zeph, an' me
not there, I'd never get over it, never. If I
was to lose him as I did Robert, I do believe it

would kill me dead." Fiercely she taunted herself with being silly; but her heart got the better
of her common sense in every such argument,
and she grew unhappier hour by hour. In this
morbid mood her thoughts also dwelt more and
more on the separation which was coming between Zeph and his children, and her doubts
grew stronger and stronger as to the possibility
of his being happy away from them. "And if
he ain't, that 'd be worse than seein' him dead, a
long ways," said the miserable Miss Sophy, tor-
turing herself to no purpose, and fighting vainly
against the pricks on all sides. "I 'd lots better
gone off an' left him here to shift for himself.
Well, there 's one thing; if worst comes to worst,
he can come back. I sha'n't keep any man from
doin' what he thinks 's right."

But fate had better things in store for Miss
Sophy than she dreamed. One night, as she had
just fallen into an uneasy sleep after lying awake
for hours grappling with these anxieties, she was

roused by the sharp ringing of the fire-bells.
Springing from her bed, she saw the whole
southern sky aglow, heard the sounds of tramp-
ling feet and hoarse cries. In a moment she
was dressed and at her door. Men and women
were running breathlessly past. In Pendar Basin
everybody went to fires; it was simply a duty
of good-fellowship, for their one fire-engine was
none too good, and the company but poorly
trained; and every hand, even a woman's hand,
counted, when it came to passing up buckets
in line.

"Where is it? What is it?" cried Miss
Sophy.

Nobody knew. "The depot," said one. "The
hotel," said another. Nobody stopped to make
sure, or to answer again; the ruddy sheets of
flame rolled up fiercer and faster; the bells rang
harder. A terrible thing is a midnight fire, even
where the best appliances of a city are close
at hand; but in a country village it seems far

crueller,—almost like a personal enemy come to slay the helpless in their sleep.

Suddenly Miss Sophy caught sound of another word. " The Star restaurant 'll go, sure," said one of the panting runners as he went by.

"My God!" cried Miss Sophy aloud; and clasping her hands she ran bareheaded into the street and looked up to the reddening sky. At that instant she felt her arm grasped violently.

" Thet restaurant's a gwine, whar she ez; it ez er judgment on 'em, I allow 't is!" cried Gammer Stein. "Come on, come on! I expect thet Zeph's thar; he'll gin his life fur her ef she's in ther fire!"

"He won't do any such thing!" cried Miss Sophy, angrily, forgetting herself, and turning on Gammer. "He ain't here; he's been gone three days!" and a prayer of thanksgiving went up from her heart. What a mercy was this! How should she be thankful enough! "Thank God, thank God!" she said in her heart, as hand in hand with Gammer she ran towards the fire.

It was indeed the Star restaurant that was "going," — going fast. The flames had already burst out of one spot in the roof; figures like black imps were seen flying past the windows; the crowd surged around the house, helplessly; shrieks, oaths, commands, confused calls, — all were blent in a terrible din, which heightened the horror of the black rolling columns of smoke and fire pouring from the windows. Vainly the little engine threw its feeble stream into the blazing mass. It quelled the flame for a second, only to let it leap up fiercer in a new spot.

In a terrible fascination Miss Sophy and Gammer pressed closer, nearer, — Miss Sophy clutching Gammer's hand in a frenzy of excitement. "Oh, where are the children? Who 's

seen the children?   Has anybody seen the children?" she shrieked.

"Burnt in their beds, I reckon," said one.
"'T ain't ten minutes since the fire burst out, 'n'
look 't that roof; it's ready to fall in now!"

"Thet's him! thet's Nat," said Gammer,
pointing to a man, blackened with smoke,
leaping from the door, bearing a desk in his
hands; back again into the flames, spite of the
warning cries of the crowd; back, and out
again, — not a drop of coward blood in Nat
Leeson's bad heart!   At that moment, just as
Miss Sophy had fastened her eyes on his face,
a scream rang out close beside her, — a scream
that no one who heard it ever forgot: "Nat!
Nat! where's the baby?"   And more like some
swift flying creature than like a human being
there came, parting the crowd right and left, as
if they had been straws in her way, the figure
of a woman, uttering shriek after shriek.   Men
tried to grasp her by the arm to hold her back.

They could no more grasp her than they could grasp the flames themselves. "Nat! Nat! where's the baby?" she shrieked. "Oh, God! save my baby! Zephie! Zephie!" Over and above all the din Nat heard the cry; and maddened as he was by terror and loss, the words seemed to turn him into a fiend. As she reached him he pushed her back, shouting hoarsely, "Damn your brat! let it burn! Good riddance!" A cry of "Shame! shame!" went up, but there was time for no further retribution. The flames were licking out of the windows now, and running up the outside walls. A few minutes would see all over. The crowd swept back a little.

"Mam, here's baby," cried a shrill, quavering voice; and out of the smoke, out of the flame, past the raging Nat, who did not even see him, tottered Zephie, bearing the baby in his arms. There went up a cheer, a short one, indeed, for the men's voices broke. They closed round the

14

boy, took the baby, lifted her; took Zephie,
lifted him. Nobody thought any longer of the
burning house; let it go; here were the children. But where was the mother? It was
some minutes before she was found. As she
tossed her arms in despair at her husband's
brutal answer to her cry, merciful unconscious-
ness had seized her, and she wavered and fell, —
fell, by the strangest of chances, into the arms
of Gammer Stein, who had pressed on closely
after her, expecting, as she afterwards confessed,
to see her plunge into the burning building and
be devoured by the flames.

"An' I allaow I wuz er thinkin' ez haow
the Lawd hed crpinted thet ther fire ez er
jedgment," she said, "'n' the next I knowed,
thar she wuz, ther pore cretur, a settlin' down
agen me, 'n' er swayin' back 'n' forth, 'n' 's
soon 's I ketched her I seen she wuz in er
dead faint; 'n' I allaow ter yeow it kind er
fetched me raound, skeered, 's ef ther Lawd

hed tuk me ter witness he wa'n't plum done
aout wi' Rushy Riker yit ! "

It was surely a strange chance which put into
the hands of Gammer Stein and Miss Sophy
the joint labor of restoring the woman to consciousness. When at last she opened her eyes
and saw Zephie in a chair opposite her, with
the child in his arms, she put her hand to her
head, and cried out pitifully, " Be we dead ?
Where 's Nat ? "

" No, no, mam," cried Zephie, holding the
baby out to her, " we ain't none of us dead !
The house 's all burnt up, but we got out. I
brought Rushy downstairs myself, 'n' the stairs
was a blazin' under me ; donno how I ever did
it ; but she never so much 's kicked nor hollered.
If she had, I 'd a dropped her sure."

" Your husband is safe too," said Miss
Sophy, with a not wholly kindly emphasis.
Miss Sophy was very human.

Snatching the baby from Zephie's arms and

straining it to her bosom, rocking herself to and fro, looking up into Gammer Stein's face wildly, Rushy exclaimed, " I wish he 'd burned up!   I never want to set my eyes on him again! "

" 'Sh, 'sh! " exclaimed Gammer; " ye donno what ye 're sayin'."

" Did ye hear what he said to me, then? " cried Rushy, bursting into a flood of hysterical crying.   " He meant to let the children burn up.   He set it afire hisself.   That 's what he sent me out o' the house for last night."

Horror-stricken, Gammer threw up her hands. Miss Sophy stood at the foot of the bed, listening intently.   They were alone with her.

" I wish God may strike me dead," cried the raving woman, " if I don't believe it!   I 'll never go nigh him again, never!   'T was to get rid o' the children he did it! "

" Rushy Riker! " exclaimed Gammer, and the old woman drew herself up till her gaunt figure seemed preternaturally tall, and, spite of her uncouth language, her utterance had the dignity of inspiration, — "Rushy Riker! yeow jest shet yer mouth, an' don't yeow tempt ther Lawd ter strike yer dead, blasphemin' thet way. Yeow air plum crazy, thet's what yer air. Yer know Nat Leeson, bad's he ez, never done nothin' er ther kind. The Lawd's gin yer both yer chillen safe 'n' sound, 'n' ye'd better git daown 'n yer knees 'n' be thankful, 'n' begin ter lead ther life ye'd oughter. 'T ain't tew late yit. Yer young; 'n' I allaow the Lawd's er dealin' 'th yeow powerful."

Rushy's great black eyes fastened on Gammer's face fiercely; the tears stopped; sobs shook her, but she did not speak. The baby, terrified, began to cry. Hushing her tenderly, cooing over her, caressing her, Rushy, with a swiftly changing face, began again to weep, but softly, as if she feared to terrify the child.

"I expect I was kind o' crazy," she muttered, "but 't aint strange."

"No," said Gammer gently, "'t ain't strange! We'll be gwine naow; yer better alone. Ther folks 'n this house said yer could hev this room till yer got time ter look raound, yeow 'n' yer — yeow 'n' Nat!" Gammer could not bring herself to speak the word "husband" in that connection. "Come, Miss Burr," she added, touching Miss Sophy on the shoulder, "we'll be gwine; we can't do nothin' more fur 'er."

Miss Sophy did not stir. She was gazing fixedly at Zephie. The child had thrown himself on the floor, and was lying with his eyes shut. "Look at him!" she whispered.

"Dew yer feel bad, Zephie?" asked Gammer. He did not answer. Bending over him, she exclaimed: "Ef thet ain't cur'us! He's sleepin'! Ain't thet a mercy, naow, he kin?" And again she drew Miss Sophy away.

Shaking off the old woman's hand, Miss Sophy stepped nearer to the bed, and said, " Mrs. Lecson, I 'd like to see you to-morrow morning. Will you be here? "

"Who be ye?" asked Rushy, half defiantly, with a distrustful glance. "I s'pose I 'll be here."

"My name is Burr," answered Miss Sophy, slowly. "You do not know me, I suppose."

"That keeps boarders?" asked Rushy.

"Yes," said Miss Sophy, trembling.

"I know where yer place is," answered Rushy, indifferently, "'n' my husband that was, he 's been workin' for you, I heered. You was the fust one 't ever got any work out o' him, I heered say."

Miss Sophy's face grew hard. It was well that the light was dim. She clenched her hands as she replied coldly, nerving herself by the thought of the purpose she had in view, "He did all the work which he did for me very well."

"Ain't he workin' on your ranch now?" asked Rushy.

"No," said Miss Sophy, thankful for the form of the question. "I 've sold my ranch."

"A good while 'fore Zeph Riker 'll get such another job!" said Rushy, vindictively.

Again Miss Sophy clenched her hands and held herself calm. For Zeph's sake nothing was too much to be borne. For the stake for which she was playing now she could afford to strain every nerve.

"Yes," she said, under all her excitement taking a certain grim satisfaction in the artful wording of her reply. "Yes, I think it will be. But I will see you in the morning, Mrs. Leeson. There 's something I want to talk to you about."

"All right," said Rushy, without a gleam of curiosity in her face. The reaction after her terrible shock was setting in; a stupor was fast stealing over her.

Miss Sophy's heart was beating high. She had hard work to keep from telling her project to Gammer Stein, but she refrained.

" Time enough if it succeeds," she said. " But it will! I know it will!"

Miss Sophy had watched Rushy's face closely while Gammer was upbraiding her for her accusation against Nat. She had seen the swift look of terror there, followed by dogged resolve, as she regained partial composure. Miss Sophy did not believe that the woman had been crazy when she uttered that accusation, or that she thought herself to have been so. Miss Sophy believed it true; and if this were so, the very strength of the poor creature's maternal affection, which had hitherto been the barrier to the carrying out of Miss Sophy's project, would be its surest aid.

Minute by minute all through the lingering darkness Miss Sophy watched for the dawn. As soon as it was fairly light, she took her way to the house. She reckoned, and rightly, that she would find Rushy alone. As she passed the still smouldering ruins of the restaurant she recognized Nat working there with a hopeless sort of fury in his motions, dragging out bits of iron and half-burnt timbers. It seemed a mockery that the chimney was left standing, and projecting from it a grate half full of coal and ashes, the remains of the last home-fire lighted on that ill-fated hearth. While she stood gazing at this, Nat pried the grate out with an iron bar; as it fell, his face was convulsed with rage, and he poured out a volley of oaths which made Miss Sophy's heart stand still.

"It was true! I believe it!" she gasped, as she quickened her pace, and did not once look back till she reached Rushy's bedside.

In the white, haggard face which looked up from the pillow half-inquiring, half-alarmed, at Miss Sophy, there were few traces left of the beauty which had been so fatal a lure to Zeph in days gone by. The year of hard work, and still more of suffering which she had been too proud to betray, had told upon Rushy sadly.

And this last night with its anguish, its dire secret, its shock, — this had completed the wreck.
She had almost the look of a dying woman.
Placid, rosy, fast asleep on her arm, lay the
child over whose destiny forces strangely conflicting were now coming together.

Miss Sophy was a keen reader of faces. As
she met Rushy's first glance she perceived in it a
defined terror. Rushy was indeed in an agony
of apprehension lest the words she had spoken
in her frenzy would be used to work harm to Nat.
She was rent between her still passionate love
for him and her mighty love for her children.

On the instant Miss Sophy changed her entire
plan of approach. This terror should be made
to play into her hands.

"Mrs. Leeson," she said gravely, "I came
down so early to be sure of seeing you before
any one else did. I suppose you remember
what you said last night about your husband's
having set his place on fire? I think no one

heard you except Gammer and me; but we
both heard you."

Rushy's eyes dilated with horror. "I was
crazy!" she cried. "I was out o' my head! I did
n't mean no such thing! Gammer said I was
crazy. She knows Nat would n't do such a thing."

"I suppose you did not know," continued
Miss Sophy, eying her steadily, — no mercy in
Miss Sophy's heart now, — "that I owned the
bakery next your restaurant?"

"No! Did ye?" gasped Rushy. "Oh, Miss
Burr, don't ye tell on me! I swear to God it
wa'n't true! I did n't know I said it! Oh, have
some mercy on me, won't ye? Nat 'd kill me
in a minute if ever he was to hear 't I 'd said
such a word. He never did it, Miss Burr,
never! Nat 's real good, he is; only jest hasty,
that 's all. Oh, for God's sake, ma'am, don't
you go to tell it!" And in anguish too great
for tears Rushy threw herself back on the bed
and groaned aloud.

"I had no idea of telling it, Mrs. Leeson,"
said Miss Sophy. "It was not for that I came.
The property was not much injured, and I am
going away. I did n't care a fig for the building. But I 'll tell you what I did come for."
Miss Sophy hesitated, bent over the bed, whispering low, "I am certain you spoke the truth
about Nat's setting that fire. I 'll never forget
your scream, never; an' I said to myself,
'There 's a woman would be glad to get her
child out o' that man's way if she could.'"
Again Miss Sophy paused. Rushy's eyes trans-
fixed her. Confession, awe, yearning, surrender, were in them.

"Oh! what be ye?" she said faintly. "Ye
scare me! What d' ye mean?"

Miss Sophy never could remember distinctly
the rest of the conversation, — how she gradually made clear to Rushy her own wish to adopt
a child; her sudden desire the night before to
take the little one whose life had been thus

endangered by her stepfather's crime; her feeling that she had been sent to the fire for this
very purpose. The words seemed to come to
her as from some power outside herself; and as
she spoke, the mother's heart seemed melted;
tears like rain ran down her face. Wringing her
hands, she said again and again, "I can't! Oh,
I can't never let her go; I'd die without her!"
And yet again and again she returned to the
point, groaning, "But I darst n't keep her! I
darst n't! I donno why I trust ye so, ma'am,
but I can't help it! I know ye won't do me no
harm; I've heard lots about ye, how good ye
was to everybody, 'n' I know ye're rich! Oh,
I'll never forgive myself if I stand 'n the child's
light 'n' keep her out o' all ye'd do for her; 'n'
I'll die if I let her go out o' my sight! 'n' there
't is!" It was a terrible struggle. More than
once Miss Sophy was on the point of abandon-
ing it. All seemed lost. Once she rose to go.
But Rushy clutched her gown and cried, "Don't

ye go! don't go! I hain't made my mind up! I can't! If it wa'n't for fearin' she ain't safe I could n't! But oh, if anythin' did happen to her here, I 'd die! I donno why Nat hates her so; he 's real good to Zephie; allers has been; but ever sence we was married he 's seemed to hate the sight o' baby. I suppose it 's hard on a man to take to another man's children; but there 's Zephie, just the same, an' he 's fond o' him."

Finally the storm-tossed creature said: " You send Gammer here; I 'll talk it over with her. I 'm spent. I can't think no longer! Gammer knows ye real well; if she says it 'll be right, I 'll do it! I 'm thankful ye 're goin' way off; that 's the only way I 'd stand it 't all. It 'll be just same 's ef she was dead; 'n' that 's the way I want it to be! I could n't give her up no other way! "

Still the baby slept on, placid, unconscious. As Miss Sophy turned to go, she bent down and kissed its forehead. " She is a most beautiful child," she said. " I love her already."

" Oh, ye 'd be good to her always, always, 's long 's ye live, and leave her safe 'n' comfortable! Oh, swear it, won't ye?" cried Rushy, hysterically. Then with a fresh outburst of crying, her words hardly articulate, she sobbed, " Should ye want her to call ye mammy? She 's just beginnin' to say it this last month or two; p'r'aps ye might let her call ye aunt, or suthin' else besides mammy!"

The anguish in the mother's voice as she said this touched a chord in Miss Sophy's breast that had never before vibrated. As tenderly and understandingly as if she herself had borne children, she answered, "Don't you think it would be best for her to call me mother? You would n't want her to grow up thinking she had no mother!"

" No, no! I s'pose she must call ye mammy. Oh, I donno but I wish she was dead now! Oh, ma'am, don't ye be angry with me! You go away now. I can't talk to ye a minute longer. Send Gammer; she'll come. She hates me, but she's good ; she'll come; she'll tell me. When are ye going?"

"To-morrow night."

"I'm glad it's so soon, — that is, if I'm goin' to do it. If I was to think it over 'n' over weeks, I should n't know no better 't the end; I'd ruther she'd go 't oncet. Gammer'll bring her ter ye. She always goes to Gammer, Zephie says. He takes her up there sometimes Sundays. I expect — " Rushy paused. Miss Sophy's instinct filled up the interval. It was of Zeph Rushy was thinking. Spite of Miss Sophy's steady nerves, she trembled now. "He hain't got no right, anyhow," Rushy muttered to herself. "The judge giv' 'em to me."

"Thar'd have to be papers, would n't there?" she said, looking up furtively, "so there could n't nobody else get her away from you?"

Miss Sophy's heart bounded. She made a feint of stooping to pick up something from the

15

floor to hide her exultation. The words, " and
mine enemy was my helper," flashed across her
thoughts.

"Yes," she replied, "that would be better.
I will send them to you by Gammer. I 'll have
a lawyer draw them up, so they will be all right;
and if you make up your mind to do it, you
can sign them, and give them to Gammer with
the baby, and I 'll have Gammer go with me
part way till the baby 's used to me."

" Swear! swear!" shrieked Rushy, snatching
Miss Sophy's hand, fastening her wild eyes
on her face. "Oh, swear to me, here 'n'
now, she 'd be t' ye the same 's yer own!
Swear!"

"So help me God," said Miss Sophy, tears
on her cheeks and her voice faltering, "she
shall be to me the same 's my own."

" I believe ye!" gasped Rushy, half fainting
from her fierce struggle. "I believe ye! I
don't never want to see ye agen, though! Don't

ye come back here. Send Gammer. If I 'll do
it, Gammer 'll bring the baby to your house.
If I don't do 't, I don't never want to be asked
no more ! Be ye sure ye 're goin' to-morrow
night ? "

"Yes," said Miss Sophy.

"South? The south-goin' train?"

"Yes," answered Miss Sophy, suddenly alive
to a new danger, and perceiving as suddenly
how it could be averted. "Yes, I am going
on the south-bound train."

"Send Gammer quick," was Rushy's only
answer; and she closed her eyes exhausted.

Even in this final crisis Miss Sophy did
not confide to Gammer her relation to Zeph.
"What folks don't know, they can't let out,"
had been Miss Sophy's motto all her life, and it
stood her in good stead now. Except for this
reticence, her plans at the last moment might
have miscarried disastrously. All that Gammer
knew when she set out on her strange embassy

was simply what had already been said by Miss
Sophy herself to Rushy. In her pocket she
carried the papers, made out in due form, by
the signing of which the legal adoption of the
child would be put forever beyond question or
revocal.

"An' I allaow she 'll sign 'em fast enough,
I allaow she will ef 't is ez she sez, accordin' ter
what I 'd 'vise her ter dew. Ther ain't no tew
sides ter ther thing; ther ez ter most things;
but I allaow ther ain't ter this," said Gammer,
as she bade Miss Sophy good-by and set out
on her errand.

It was arranged between them that if Gammer
obtained the child she would pass Miss Sophy's
house on her way home, Miss Sophy watching
at the window to see if she had been successful.
In that case Gammer was to keep the child
with her until the next evening, when she would
bring her to the train, joining Miss Sophy there
at the last moment. Miss Sophy's brain ached

with all this plotting and planning, so foreign to her straightforward nature. She felt disgraced in her own eyes by so much concealment. "Lord knows I'll be thankful to get done with all this coverin'-up business," she reflected. "It's a new trade for me; but then, I'm takin' up a new trade altogether," — and her face softened into a younger look at the very thought. "It's all for his sake I'm doin' it. Once we're out o' this country 'n' settled down, it won't seem nothin' at all; 'n' I know 't's right! that's one comfort."

It was late in the afternoon before Gammer, equipped with the paper ready for Rushy's signature, and already signed by Miss Sophy, set out on her exciting errand. Never before in Gammer's life had she been called upon to take part in such stirring events. But she bore herself like a veteran, and had no misgivings as to the success of the enterprise. The only thing that puzzled her was the mysterious secrecy in which Miss Sophy insisted on wrapping the whole affair.

"Thar ain't no disgrace 'n 'doptin' er child," she reflected. "I allaow 't 's ter ennybody's cheeriterble credit ter feel ter dew it; but Miss Burr ez fur coverin' 't up ez much ez ef 't wuz er case er stealin'. I allaow she's drefful afeard o' folks talkin', bein' an old maid 's she ez; 'n' thar's plenty 't would talk, 'n' kinder larf; folks ez jest mean enuf. It's different, her bein' 'n old maid. Naow ef 't wuz me, nobody'd say er word. Old maids hez er hard time, ennyway; 'pears like thar shet out er lots o' things, 'sides not hevin' no man o' ther own."

The minutes seemed hours to Miss Sophy as she sat at her window gazing down the street by which Gammer would return. The sun went slowly down toward the mountain-tops, reached them, seemed to linger a moment, then sank, and was gone; then the slow twilight passed, and dusky gloom settled on the little town.

There was no moon; Miss Sophy could see but a few paces beyond her gate. No Gammer yet!

She could not bear it. Throwing a shawl over her head, she stole out and paced up and down in the path. At last she saw the tall figure looming up in the distance, walking with a swift stride, — too swift to be the step of one carrying the burden of a heavy child.

Miss Sophy stood still. As soon as she saw that the old woman's arms were empty, she ran forward, exclaiming under her breath, "Would n't she do it? Oh, what shall I do! What shall I do!"

"Hesh, naow," said Gammer, as composedly as if it were an every-day transaction over which Miss Sophy excited herself unnecessarily. "Don' git yerself inter er fever! She's gwine ter; she's signed; but she don't want ter giv her up till ther last minute; she wants ter fix her up; she hain't got no cloes fit ter go in,

she sez. I declar ter yeow, Miss Burr, I did n't
never allaow ter feel ez near kind ter Rushy
Riker ez I dew. Thet 's what 's kep' me. 'T
seemed ter kind er dew her sum good ter talk.
She sed she allers knowed I war daown on her,
an' I war; but she 's broke naow. But ez I ben
tellin' her, she 's made her bed 'n' she 's got ter
lay in 't, this time; 'n' I allaow it 's a hard un.
She 's 'feard 's death o' thet Nat, — 'feard 's
death; 'n' yit she kinder doos love him tew;
she won't never leave him ser long 's the breath
er life 's in her body; she darst n't; she sez he 'd
kill ennybody in a minnit, 'n' not mean ter,
nuther; when he 's inter his rages he donno
nothin'. I allaow she 's got inter hell afore her
time, she hez! Thet 's the way ye 've got ther
baby; she 'd ha' died afore she 'd parted 'th her,
ef 't hed n't been jest 's 't is. Yeow 'd hev pitied
her ef ye 'd seen her tryin' to sign thet paper,
yeow would. 'T seemed 's ef she could n't do 't.
She 'd put ther pen daown, 'n' then she 'd pick 't

up; 'n' ther paper's all riz up in blotches whar she cried on 't 'n' tried ter wipe 't off 'th her gown, 'n' 't made 't wuss. Yeow 'd hev pitied her."

"No, I would n't!" replied Miss Sophy. "I have n't got any pity for a woman that does what she 's done."

Gammer drew a long sigh. It was too dark for her to see Miss Sophy's face. They were standing close together in the shadow of a tree, whispering like conspirators.

"Yeow 'd hev ter, ef yer seen her," she said; "not but what she 's reapin' ez she sowed; I ain't er gainsayin' thet; 'n' I allaow ther Lawd 's gwine ter punish her wuss yit 'fore He 's done 'th her."

"How?" said Miss Sophy.

"I allaow she 's gwine ter break all ter pieces. She 's jest ther high-strung kind thet doos; she 's all uv er tremble; narves ez awful when they gits broke up thet way. She sez she knows she 's gwine ter die, 'n' she don't care how soon; 'n' I say, ther sooner ther better, tew; fur thet Nat, he won't keer fur her a minnit when she 's lost her looks 'n' can't cook, — not er minnit; he 's thet kind. Naow thet Zeph, he 'd hev — "

" Are you sure she will give you the child to-morrow? " interrupted Miss Sophy. She could not bear any reference to Zeph in this connection.

" Sure 's I am 't I 'm erlive," answered Gammer. " She 's a gwine ter bring her up ter-morrer arter she 's hed her supper, 'n' she 'll git her ter sleep ter my house. I allaow ter yeow I dread ter see her go 'n' leave her. I allaowed mebbe she 'd better come down ter ther train; but — "

" Oh," shrieked Miss Sophy, " don't let her! She 'd be sure to take it all back at the last minute. Don't let her!" And Miss Sophy actually quivered with alarm.

"She won't come thar," answered Gammer. "She allaowed she could n't. She allaowed she'd die when she heered the whistle, 's 't wuz. She sez it's a comfort ter her I 'm goin' part way. Not thet she's got enny kind er distrust o' yeow; but ther baby knows me, 'n' she's a sckeery little thing. I allaow yeow 'll have trouble 'th her along fur a spell."

"I think not," said Miss Sophy, with a joy at her heart, thinking of the baby nestled in its father's arms. "I 'm not afraid."

After they had parted, Gammer turned back, calling cautiously, "Oh, Miss Burr, I clar fur-got! She's powerful 'fraid Zeph 'll get wind on 't somehow 'n' interfere. I allaowed ter her he 'd ruther yeow hed ther baby 'n enny woman livin'; he knowed yer; but she ain't easy 'bout it. Whar is Zeph naow? D' yer know? We hain't seed him for a week back."

"He went into the country on business for me," replied Miss Sophy.

"'Ll he be back 'fore yer go?"

"I expect him to-morrow; at least, that was the plan. But he may be detained," said the guilty Miss Sophy.

"Ef he doos come, ye kin tell him all abaout it yerself," replied the unsuspecting Gammer, "'n' he'll be thankful ter ther Lawd, I allaow he will."

"I hope he will," ejaculated Miss Sophy, fervently. And as she ran home she said to herself, "I hope to the Lord that's the last manouverin' I'll have to do till my dyin' day. It's awful wearin'. I shouldn't wonder if it's worse 'n out-'n'-out lyin'!"

VII.

THE simple ceremony which had made Miss Sophy and Zeph "man and wife," as the customary phrase strangely words it, was over. The minister and his wife, who had known Miss Sophy ever since her coming into the town, respected her, and trusted her as a stanch friend, were nevertheless disquieted by this last act of hers, and by the seemingly clandestine way in which she had insisted upon having it performed.

"If she wa'n't ashamed of it, what'd she want to come in here to be married, just like a servant-girl?" said the wife. "I'd never believed it o' Sophy Burr, never!" And the minister had replied thoughtfully, "It does seem queer; but

Miss Sophy 's always got some good reason for what she does; that poor Riker 's been through such dreadful troubles here, I don't wonder she does n't want it talked about."

" She 's just thrown herself away, that 's what it is," said the wife.

" I hope not," replied the minister, still more thoughtfully. " There 's something noble in the man's look, sad as 't is. He 'll come up yet. Sophy Burr 's no fool."

Meantime the two thus being discussed were standing hand in hand just outside the parsonage gate. Strange words to be spoken by bride and bridegroom within five minutes of the ceremony which had made them one were passing between them.

" Zeph," said Sophy, the instant they had passed the gate, — " Zeph, I 've got to do something now that 'll try you considerable; but you must trust me. You 've got to let me walk alone down to the depot and get into the cars

by myself, and you get into the last car and
stay there till I come t' ye. 'T won't be
long —"

"Sophy!" interrupted Zeph, half alarmed,
half angry, "what notion 's taken ye to do
that? I don't think it 's decent, Sophy. What
'll folks think? It 's dark; ye need n't be afraid
o' folks seein' us 's we go along. They 've got
to know it to-morrow morning; they might as
well know it to-night."

It had been a sore point to Zeph already, the
secrecy in which their plans had been shrouded.
Humble-minded and self-distrustful as he was,
he was also sensitive to a fault; and he had
spent many a wretched hour, needlessly tortur-
ing himself with the question if it could be that
the faithful and devoted Sophy felt shame of
having linked her fortunes with his.

"If you 'd heard me through," retorted
Sophy, brusque even in this supreme moment
of her life, " you 'd have seen that it was n't any

notion, nor nothin' like a notion. It's got to be done, Zeph, an' you've got to trust me. I've got a reason, an' if you knew it you would n't ask me to do different. You'd help me all you could, an' not make me feel bad either. Can't ye trust me 's long 's one hour, Zeph? I'd do it for you. Trust me, Zeph. I'm your wife now, you know!"

"Of course I'll trust ye, Sophy," replied Zeph, half appeased, but only half. "It was n't no question o' trustin', an' I'll do jest as you want me to; hain't I always? But I don't see why ye can't tell me what 't is, Sophy."

"Oh, dear!" she cried hysterically, "we have n't got any time to lose, standin' here; it's 'most train-time now. I can't tell you! an' when you know what 't is, you 'll see I could n't tell you. You 'll be real glad I did n't, Zeph. Oh, do trust me! you 've got to!" — she was crying now, — "for I'm goin' right off this minute!" And with a convulsive clasp of her husband's hand she turned and walked away at the top of her speed. Tears ran down her cheeks, and in her excitement she talked aloud to herself as she ran: "If she should take it into her head to come down there! If she was to see Zeph, she might suspect! Perhaps she's backed out already! Perhaps Gammer won't get down there in time! Supposin' Zeph did n't take notice o' my tellin' him to get into the last car!"

The fast-multiplying terrors so unnerved her, that she felt for the first time in her sturdy life faint, — which but added another alarm. "If I should be fool enough to go an' faint, I should give up!" she said. The self-contempt she felt at this thought proved the best of tonics, and by the time she reached the railway station she was almost herself again.

It wanted only ten minutes of the train-time, but there was a sleepy expression about every-

body and everything at the station which struck
fear to her heart. "Train's late, I'll be bound,"
she thought.

Yes, the train was late; only an hour, though.
That would soon pass. In a few moments she
saw a tall figure, much wrapped and encum-
bered, coming over a low hill to the north of the
station. A short cross-cut from Gammer Stein's
house would run that way. Her breath coming
thick and fast, Miss Sophy stepped towards the
figure. It was Gammer, and she held the child
in her arms. At the sight, Miss Sophy felt
herself again in danger of fainting. "I didn't
know I'd got it in me to be so upset," she
thought, as she laid her hand on Gammer's
shoulder, and tried to speak. "You've got
her!" was all she could say.

"Yes," whispered Gammer, "she's asleep.
I jest giv' her ther leastest bit er paregoric;
't won't hurt her er mite; 'n' I put er li'le bottle
on 't inter ther bundle, already sweetened. Yer

need n't be er mite afeerd ter give it ter her ef she hollers."

"The train's late!" said Miss Sophy, clutching Gammer's arm. "We'll have to walk about. Keep out here 'n the shade."

"Ain't thet drefful, naow," said Gammer. "I allaowed ter git hyar jest on ther minnit, five minnits erhead er time, so 's ter git right on board. It 's lucky I giv' her the paregoric. But she 's powerful heavy. I allaow ter yeow my arm 's plum broke!"

"Let me take her," said Miss Sophy; and a warm glow kindled in her breast as the unconscious little creature was laid in her arms.

Zeph was peering anxiously in every direction. He too had discovered that the train was late; but that did not console him for his wife's non-appearance, since she could not have known that fact, and ought long before this to have been on the platform. Dire anxiety consumed him. Where was she? What did it mean? He

saw the two dimly outlined figures pacing up
and down in the distance; but in contrast with
Gammer's great height, Sophy's figure looked
so short, he did not dream of its being hers;
and besides, that figure was carrying a child.
He did not give it a second look.

The hour had nearly passed. The sleepy,
waiting passengers outside on the benches and
in the waiting-room were beginning to bestir
themselves; trucks were being wheeled, luggage
moved, carriages driving up. Walking boldly
forward now, Zeph scrutinized all. No Sophy
to be seen! Just as he was on the point of
turning away, with the resolve that come what
might he would not get into the train till he
had seen her, his eye was arrested by a swift-
running figure, — a woman, crossing the track
a few rods from the station and turning towards
it. A signal-lantern, hung high on a derrick,
flashed its light full upon her as she passed. It
was Rushy, her face wild, her hair dishevelled.

"My God!" gasped Zeph. "That's what Sophy was afraid of! That's Rushy, and she's drunk! I'll hide, 'n' do jest's Sophy told me to. She's got some plan o' gettin' aboard herself; she had a reason, sure enough! But she might ha' told me!"

Beyond the track, on the side farthest from the station, was a gulch thick grown with weeds and young cottonwood trees. Into this Zeph leaped, and stood waiting for the train; as soon as it pulled in he sprang to the platform of the rear car, and entering it, sank into a seat. Whatever came now, he at least had fulfilled to the letter his wife's request. But the suspense was beyond his endurance.

"It'd kill Sophy if she was to make a row 'n' insult her," he said, "'n' me not there to stand by her!" And going out on the platform, he leaned out, straining his eyes forward along the train, just in time to see Sophy standing back from the steps of the forward car and assisting an elderly woman burdened with a child in her arms to get in before her.

"Just like Sophy," he thought, "always helpin' somebody! Oh, why don't she jump in quick? Where 's Rushy? She was a lookin' to see me, I expect, an' so she 's missed her!"

It had been but five minutes, — only an insignificant way-station stop; but it had settled the life-destiny of more than one human being.

The unfortunate Rushy was coming to the station on a very different errand from that which Zeph had suspected. In fact, she did not reach the station at all. If he had watched for a moment longer he would have seen her pause, look attentively at the crowd gathered there, and then, retreating into the darkness, seat herself on the ground at the base of a telegraph-pole, against which she leaned in an attitude of despair.

Her house was not far distant from the railway station, and as the time approached for the train to pass, the poor creature had pressed her face against the window, listening for the whistle and looking for the light. Becoming alarmed at length by the long delay, she had run bare-headed to the station to find what it meant. Seeing the waiting crowd, she had understood at once, and had thrown herself on the ground, resolved not to leave the place till the train had come and gone. No thought of withdrawing from her agreement or even of looking again on the face of her child had been in her mind. On the contrary, her resolve had strengthened hourly since her interview with Miss Sophy; but the strengthening of her resolve did not diminish the intensity of her grief.

"It 'll kill me, I know 't will," was the constant refrain in her thoughts; always following it, however, "but I 'll never forgive myself if I don't do it. I darst n't not do 't!"

Sobbing aloud in the safe shelter of the darkness, she watched each movement in the con-

fusion at the train, vainly trying to distinguish
the form of Miss Sophy or of Gammer. The
moments which seemed so long to all the other
actors in the drama seemed to her like lightning seconds.

"Oh, they 're goin'!" she cried, as the train
began to move. "Oh, God, she 's gone!
Baby!" and she fell back senseless on the
earth.

At that moment Zeph was saying to himself,
"Thank God, we 're safe off!" and Miss Sophy,
devoutly, "Thank God, she did n't come down!"
and Gammer, aloud, taking Miss Sophy's hand
in hers, "What ails yer? Yer tremblin' like a
leaf!"

"I 've got something to tell you, Gammer,"
replied Miss Sophy, in a whisper; and she told
her then, at last, the truth.

It was well that the necessity of carrying on
their conversation in a cautious whisper re-
strained Gammer from the full expression of

her emotions; but the repression of them was almost beyond her power. Disjointed and incredulous ejaculations were at first all which could take shape in her thought; then followed an avalanche of questions, some of them hard to answer; but soon all else was swallowed up in a heartfelt sympathy and gladness which were comforting to Miss Sophy's heart.

"You don't think 't was wrong, then, not to let her know who she was givin' her to, do you?" said Miss Sophy.

"Nerry bit of it!" replied Gammer. "'Twa'n't no use runnin' ther resk on 't. I donno haow she 'd hev tuk it. Mebbe she 'd hev been willin'er, 'n' mebbe not ser willin'. Thar ain't no countin' on folks; yer can't never tell. I sh'd allaow she 'd been willin'er; but then agin she might er tuk a jealous fit 'n' thar would n't hev been any doin' nothin'. 'T 's best 's 't is. Ye 've managed wonderful, I allaow yeow hev; 'n' naow ther sooner yer let thet pore Zeph know she 's hyar ther better. I allaow he 's 'most crazy, settin' thar waitin'!"

"Oh," faltered Miss Sophy, "I did n't mean to tell him till we got out of the train! I don't want to have any kind o' fuss in the cars."

"He won't make no fuss," replied Gammer. "He ain't thet

———

HERE the story of Zeph comes to an abrupt ending. Conceived and begun by Mrs. Jackson in Los Angeles during the winter of 1884–1885, it was put by to be finished on her arrival home in Colorado Springs,—a home she was destined never to reach. In her last hours she sent the manuscript to her publisher with this message: —

I am very sorry I cannot finish "Zeph." Perhaps it is not worth publishing in its unfinished state, as the chief lesson for which I wrote it was to be forcibly told at the end. You must be judge about this. I suppose there will be some interest in it as the last thing I wrote. I will make a short outline of the plot of the close of the story. . . . Good-by. Many thanks for all your long good-will and kindness. I shall look in on your new rooms some day, be sure — but you won't see me. Good-by.

Affectionately forever,

H. J.

AUGUST 7.

On a separate sheet was the " Outline."

THE CLOSE OF "ZEPH."

THEY were to settle down on a ranch in one of the beautiful cañons in South California, opening out seaward, yet not so near the water as to be too cold for fruits. I had the precise spot in my memory,— an ideal nook, apricots and vineyards, cherry-trees in bloom there in March, tomatoes ripe on the hillsides in January; a glimmer of sea to be seen from the mouth of the cañon fourteen miles away, — endless charm to Miss Sophy, half-sad spell to Zeph. At the end of two years, one night as she is watching the sunset light on the water from one of the hills at the mouth of their cañon, she looks down and sees Zeph coming up the road with his arm around a boy's waist. It is Zephie. His mother is dead, — had saved enough money for him to come to South California and join his father. She had learned of the marriage, and as soon as Gammer returned there was a stormy scene; but she soon grew reconciled, and finally glad. As Gammer had predicted, she never recovered her strength, but pined away in a mysterious nervous break-down. Zephie's story is pathetic. The stepfather was never "bad" to her, but never "real good;" the boy was her only comfort. Whenever she could save a dollar, she sent it by Zephie to Gammer to keep, and made Gammer promise to see him safe started for California. A letter from Gammer sent by Zephie told the details of the last hours, when the poor woman said she died easier, thinking how forgiving Zeph had been to her; that she thought if a *man* could forgive her like that, perhaps Christ would forgive her too! " She allaowed," said Gammer, " thet she could n't never hev got no faith to die trustin', ef it hed n't ben fur ther way Zeph 'd allers kep' on er furgivin' her, time an' agen; 'n' she jest trusted God 'd be ez good ter her ez Zeph wuz!"

" Now," said Miss Sophy in her heart, " at last, Zeph 'll have real peace and comfort. He 's never felt settled in his mind yet, and he never would 's long 's he had n't got the boy; 'n' I don't know 's he would 's long 's she was above ground! But there won't be a happier man in all California than he 'll be now! " And a flush born of a secret known only to Miss Sophy's own heart was red on her cheek as she went to the door and called her husband and his boy in to supper.

RAMONA: A Story.

By HELEN JACKSON (H. H.).

12mo. Cloth. Price $1.50.

The Atlantic Monthly says of the author that she is "a Murillo in literature," and that the story "is one of the most artistic creations of American literature." Says a lady: "To me it is the most distinctive piece of work we have had in this country since 'Uncle Tom's Cabin,' and its exquisite fiuish of style is beyond that classic." "The book is truly an American novel," says the *Boston Advertiser*. "Ramona is one of the most charming creations of modern fiction," says Charles D. Warner. "The romance of the story is irresistibly fascinating," says *The Independent*.

"The best novel written by a woman since George Eliot died, as it seems to me, is Mrs. Jackson's 'Ramona.' What action is there! What motion! How *entrainant* it is! It carries us along as if mounted on a swift horse's back, from beginning to end, and it is only when we return for a second reading that we can appreciate the fine handling of the characters, and especially the Spanish mother, drawn with a stroke as keen and firm as that which portrayed George Eliot's 'Dorothea.'" — *T. W. Higginson, in Harper's Bazar.*

Unsolicited tribute of a stranger, a lady in Wisconsin: —

"I beg leave to thank you with an intense heartiness for your public espousal of the cause of the Indian. In your 'Century of Dishonor' you showed to the country its own disgrace. In 'Ramona' you have dealt most tenderly with the Indians as men and women. You have shown that their stoicism is not indifference, that their squalor is not always of their own choosing. You have shown the tender grandeur of their love, the endurance of their constancy. While, by 'Ramona,' you have made your name immortal, you have done something which is far greater. You are but one: they are many. You have helped those who cannot help themselves. As a novel, 'Ramona' must stand beside 'Romola,' both as regards literary excellence and the portrayal of life's deepest, most vital, most solemn interests. I think nothing in literature since Goldsmith's 'Vicar of Wakefield' equals your description of the flight of Ramona and Alessandro. Such delicate pathos and tender joy, such pure conception of life's realities, and such loftiness of self-abnegating love! How much richer and happier the world is with 'Ramona' in it!"

Sold by all booksellers. Mailed, post-paid, by the publishers,

ROBERTS BROTHERS, Boston.

A KEY TO " RAMONA."

A CENTURY OF DISHONOR.

A Sketch of the United States Government's Dealings with some of the Indian Tribes.

By HELEN JACKSON (H. H.),

AUTHOR OF "RAMONA," "VERSES," "BITS OF TRAVEL," ETC.

A New Edition. 12mo. pp. 514. Cloth. $1.50.

"The report made by Mrs. Jackson and Mr. Kinney is grave, concise, and deeply interesting. It is added to the appendix of this new edition of her book. In this California journey, Mrs. Jackson found the materials for ' Ramona,' the Indian novel, which was the last important work of her life, and in which nearly all the incidents are taken from life. In the report of the Mission Indians will be found the story of the Temecula removal and the tragedy of Alessandro's death as they appear in ' Ramona.' " — *Boston Daily Advertiser.*

" A number of striking cases of breach of faith, heartless banishment from homes confirmed to the Indians by solemn treaties, and wars wantonly provoked in order to make an excuse for dispossessing them of their lands, are grouped together, making a panorama of outrage and oppression which will arouse the humanitarian instincts of the nation to the point of demanding that justice shall be done toward our savage wards. . . . 'H. H.' succeeds in holding up to the public eye a series of startling pictures of Indian wrongs, drawn from a century of American history." — *New York Tribune.*

Mrs. Jackson's Letter of Gratitude to the President.

The following letter from Mrs. Jackson to the President was written by her four days before her death, Aug. 12, 1885 : —

To GROVER CLEVELAND, *President of the United States:*

Dear Sir, — From my death-bed I send you a message of heartfelt thanks for what you have already done for the Indians. I ask you to read my " Century of Dishonor." I am dying happier for the belief I have that it is your hand that is destined to strike the first steady blow toward lifting this burden of infamy from our country, and righting the wrongs of the Indian race.

With respect and gratitude,

HELEN JACKSON.

Sold by all booksellers. Mailed, post-paid, on receipt of price, by the publishers,

ROBERTS BROTHERS, BOSTON.

www.ingramcontent.com/pod-product-compliance
Lightning Source LLC
Chambersburg PA
CBHW020851270326
41928CB00006B/648